AFRICAN AMERICAN HERITAGE

BY

DAVID TUESDAY ADAMO Rel.D; Ph.D

Resource *Publications*
An imprint of *Wipf and Stock Publishers*
150 West Broadway • Eugene OR 97401

Resource *Publications*
an imprint of Wipf and Stock Publishers
150 West Broadway
Eugene, Oregon 97401

African American Heritage
By Adamo, David Tuesday
©2001 Adamo, David Tuesday
ISBN: 1-57910-684-6
Publication date: July, 2001
Previously published by Texian Press, 2001.

TABLE OF CONTENTS

Dedication... ii
Acknowledgements..iii

INTRODUCION 1

HISTORICAL HERITAGE 7

THE RELIGIOUS HERITAGE...41
Inseparability of Religious from Secular 41
Ancestors' Religion..57
Biblical Heritage..68

THE CULTURAL HERITAGE..78
Music..78
Dance..88
The Concept of Time 92
Name-Giving 96

CONCLUSION..104
SELECTED BIBLIOGRAPHY..105

DEDICATION

This book is dedicated to my Late Mother,
Osayomi Anugbegun Adamo
and my Late Brother
Daniel Atesogun Adamo

ACKNOWLEDGEMENTS

My special appreciation goes to the following people who have been influential, through their encouragement and editorial assistance, in bringing this book to completion: Mr. James Bola Obielodan, Department of Church and State, Baylor University, Waco, Texas; Ms. Pauline Nolly Logan (Registered Dietician) Department of Food and Drug Administration, Dallas, Texas. I am grateful to my son, Yomi Adamo who went through the manuscript.

CHAPTER ONE

Introduction

Problem of Terminology

I have examined such names as "Negro," "Black American," and "Afro-American," and I am very dissatisfied with them. I am dissatisfied with them for the racist and inferiority concept they carried with them. This will be seen as we examine their meaning below:

Black American

A close examination of the definition of "black" and "white" in the *Webster's New World Dictionary* will definitely persuade any reader that the term "Black-American" is questionable and therefore should be rejected. According to Webster,[1] "black" means "burn," "gleam," "having dark-colored skin and hair," "totally without light; in complete darkness," "very dark," "soiled," "dirty," "evil," "wicked," "harmful, " "disgraceful, " full of sorrow or suffering, " "sad; dismal; gloomy," "disastrous," "without hope," etc. Among the definitions given to "white" by Webster[2] are "opposite of black," "very blond," morally or spiritually pure; spotless; innocent; free from evil intent; harmless;" "Caucasoid," etc.

Negro

The term "Negro" is Spanish Portuguese; with its derivation from the Latin word "Niger." Both the Spanish-Portuguese and Latin terms mean "black." The French word "Noir" and the Italian "Nero" have their derivation from the same Latin word "Niger." Around the Sixteenth Century C.E., the Spanish-Portuguese term made its way to the English language. This term was first applied to the Africans living South of Egypt. Unfortunately, the term "Negro" which means "black," actually describes neither Africans nor African American people. They have several shades of complexion. Africa, one's complexion does not in any way have ethnic significance. This term "Negro" should be totally rejected, not only because it describes neither Africans nor

Introduction

African-Americans, but also because the term means "black." As stated above, the term "black," symbolizes, not only ugliness, but also evil, wickedness, sadness, disgrace and hopelessness, according to Weber's New World Dictionary. Perhaps, the term "Negro" and 'Black-American were given to the Africans and the African-American people for the ugliness and the sadistic meaning they represent. This may be believed if one looks back to the period when Africans and African-Americans were regarded as less than human.[3]

Afro-American

People of Italian ancestry are called Italian-American and not "Ita-American;" those of Jewish ancestry are called Jewish-Americans and not Je-American; " those of Japanese ancestry are called Japanese-American and not "Jap-American;" those of German ancestry are called German-American and not "Ger-American." Why in the world are the people of African ancestry called Afro-Americans instead of African-Americans? It is my opinion that the term Afro-American should be discarded and replaced with "African American." The term "Afro-American" fails to give full identification to the exact historical place from which the Africans who came to the United States originated. The term "African-American will be used throughout this book instead of Negro, Black American, and Afro American, because it does not accurately indicate the origin of African Americans and avoids racist and unpleasant connotations forced on them by the slavers.

Fallacies About African-American Past

Many fallacies have been formulated in the course of history to validate the idea that African Americans (and "black" people as a whole) are an inferior stock of people. These fallacies (myths) were outlined by Melville J. Herskovits in his book, The Myth of the Negro Past.[4]

1. That in contrast to the American Indians who preffered death to slavery, the African-Americans have childlike character and accept easily and happily -the most unsatisfactory social situations."

2. That only the "poorer stock of Africans was taken into slavery, because the clever ones were clever enough to escape the slave raids.

Introduction

3. That the Africans who were brought from Africa have lost all their tribal identity and culture, since they were brought from different areas of the continent and were scattered all over America.

4. That the Africans who were brought actually gave up their African tradition because those traditions were so savage and "so low in the scale of civilization" when compared with the superiority of the culture of the white masters and that inferior African customs are not worth remembering.

5. That the African-Americans therefore have no history, no past, and no culture.

6. That their ancestors in Africa hated them and that was why they sold them as slaves to the white man.

7. That the Africans and African-American people are not human beings, but like dogs and Kudus.[5]

Every teaching, both at home and in schools, has been shaped toward the perpetuation of this idea that people called "black" are inferior. This is most obvious on television programs when these people are portrayed as either stupid or savage. The series, Tarzan, of ten portrayed Africans as either helpless or savage. Even now, the effort to support these fallacies continues. Some so-called scientists, falsifying-scientific data, claim that African-American people are genetically inferior. Many colleges and universities still support the belief that the only thing the African-American people can do successfully is to entertain. As a result, most African-American students are admitted only for athletic purposes. Unfortunately, even some African-American scholars such as E. F. Frazier and E. B. Reuter, who are influenced by these fallacies believe that all traces of Africanism have been lost by the African-Americans in the course of capture, importation, and enslavement.[6] Of course, one must under stand why some African-American people discounted their heritage. (1) Many great cultural and religious accomplishments of African people have not been made known to the western World at large; (2) the image of Africans and African-Americans presented on television, in movies, and in books has been unfavorable; (3) many of the past experiences of African Americans have been bitterly painful and finally,

Introduction

(4) African-Americans have been accorded low status in the United States, as evident from the fallacies already mentioned above. But is it true that the African people who were kidnapped, captured, and forced to come to America are those of inferior stock? Did their ancestors hate them and therefore sold them to the White man? Did they originally have any unique heritage? Have they lost all traces of these heritages as some scholars have claim? If they have heritages, are these heritages still apparent in their present behavior? Although one must sympathize with those ideas that African-American people have lost all their African heritage African influences on African-American behavior are evident.

Contrary to the above fallacies, African-American ancestors have made great contribution to world civilizations and culture. Most scientists, eminent anthropologists and archaeologists, agree that African-American ancestors were first of all humankind, thus human life began in Africa. African-American ancestors originated religion, the art of writing and civilization. Although some modern scholars, overwhelmed with scholastic racism, have denied it, the Greek scholars such as Diodorus and others, did not hesitate, to affirm that African American ancestors are first, the originator of civilization, originator of the art of writing (hieroglyphics), religion, and science. There was a period when African-American ancestors ruled the entire known world. This period was referred to by one outstanding scholar as an "astonishing epoch of Nigger domination."[7] Despite the untold opposition, the distinctive historical, cultural and religious heritage is visible in the daily activities of the *African American p*eople in United States.

Although the above questions have been partly answered in several books and essays, some of these works are not readily available to the general public. They are written in such a technical language that it is very difficult for the general reader to understand them. Specifically, I have found valuable information in these "scholarly" works is little known to the average African American readers. Moreover, I know of nowhere in which some of this information about African-American heritage has been into a systematic, simple order for the majority of African-American readers.

In my investigation, it appeared that everywhere I went, almost every child of German-Americans knew that his/her ancestors are Germans; every American-Jewish child knew that his/her ancestors are Jewish; every Italian-American child knew that his/her ancestors are Italians. Every Chinese-American child knew that his/her ancestors are Chinese. But among the African-Americans, many parents did not even

Introduction

know, much less their children, that they have African ancestors. I felt there is an urgent need for some simple information to be made available to these people. In order for the African-American people to be proud of themselves and their identity, it is important to know from where they came, who they are, and why they behave the way they behave.

Purpose

The purpose of this book, therefore, is to provide a non-technical, straightforward book, mainly for popular readers, which provides relevant information about the African-American heritage. Although it might be valuable for a scholarly audience, the simplicity, and the brevity of facts are designed for average readers. The uniqueness of this book is that it is written by an African who was born in African continent and has lived long enough in both worlds (United States and Africa) to have clearly observed the behavior and culture of African American people.

In this book, it is not my task to do either a rigorous, comparative study of African Traditional Religion (ATR) and the African American Christianity, or the African-American history of the United States and African. Such has been demonstrated in some of the scholarly books referred to above. But there is a need for a fresh simple, unsophisticated approach, so that the general public may be aware of these valuable facts. There is also a need for a restatement of the African-American historical, religious, and cultural heritage until every African-American mothers and fathers and their children are aware of such rich heritage, which belongs to them. This will enable them to be proud of their identity, their history, and their culture, knowing that God has brought them from a long way. It is my hope that every African American minister would grasp this book, read it, and pass the information on to their audience, since they are the most authoritative custodians of both religious, political, and cultural life of the African Americans. Therefore, Africans and African American scholars must not rest until these facts are adequately known, not only to the black audience, but also to the white audience who may care to know, so that they may not misrepresent their neighbors as a result of ignorance, and thus bear false witness against them (Exod 20:16).

Although there is no clear-cut division between a religious and cultural heritage for the sake of simplicity and understanding, the book is divided into four main chapters. The first chapter is the general introduction to the book. The second chapter deals with the historical

Introduction

heritage. It contains a general historical achievement of the African-American ancestors. Their presence in America before Columbus ever dreamed of coming to America, and the post-Columbus history of the coming of the African-American people will be briefly examined.

The third chapter deals with the religious heritage of African Americans, with special emphasis on the characteristics of religion among Africans and African Americans in the United States. These section has also been expanded to include the traditional religion and biblical heritage of African American ancestors.

Chapter four examines the cultural heritage of the African Americans, with emphasis on music, concept of time, and name giving. This section on music and name giving has been enlarged. It is my hope Africans and African American scholars would continue to put their observations in simple written form.

While reading this book, it is important for my readers to suspend some of the traditional teaching about Africans and African Americans by the slave masters.

CHAPTER II

AFRICAN AMERICAN
HISTORICAL HERITAGE

Readers may wonder why we are preoccupied with the past instead of focusing our attention on the present and the future. Why is it necessary to know the past history of the African-Americans when the past was so unpleasant for them? Why are the majority of them presently suffering and the future does not seem to offer any hope? These are fundamental questions, which are rooted in the experience of the African-American people. They are questions, which challenge the relevance of history, especially the history of Africans and African-American people.

Historical Heritage

Professor Maulana Karenga has done a marvelous job in bringing out the basic relevance of history, which I think will serve as basic answers to the above question.[8]

Firstly, history is "a source of self-understanding." In this case, the study of the African-American historical, cultural and religious heritage "becomes a solution to the identity question in terms of their historical origin and achievement." History unquestionably points to Africa as the place of origin of the African-Americans in the United States of America. It reveals that the people called "Negro," 'Black-Americans," and "Afro-Americans" have African identity. They have "heirs of unsurpassed historical legacy which effectively ends the need to try to identify." themselves with other races.[9] Knowing their history and their heritage opens "possibilities of future, national and world achievement, based on what they have achieved in the past.[10]

Secondly, the study of the past historical heritage of the African American people will enable them to understand the society and the world. It will enable African-Americans to understand society's behavior; namely, why records were hidden, "distorted, and destroyed by slaveholders."

Thirdly, history reveals a measure of people's humanity, for" history and humanity are inseparable." To deny the historical achievements of certain people is to deny them their humanity.[11] Why did the slaveholders forbid the teaching of African-American people to read or write during the time of slavery? It was meant to prevent them from discovering their history and their humanity in contrast to the slaveholders' fallacies that the African-American people were less human. When we study our heritage, we rescue and reconstruct our humanity by challenging, disproving, and correcting the fallacies imposed on the Africans and the African-American people. Thus the African-Americans are able to know and affirm the fact that their ancestors are the initiators of western civilization.[12]

Finally, history serves as "a source of models to emulate." When African-American people know and affirm their heritage, that heritage serves as a foundation to build upon; it serves for future achievement as an example to follow.

Thus, the study of African American heritage is indispensable, for history is still present with us. It is still affecting the Africans and African Americans, consciously and unconsciously. Our history tells us that we have been successful people and we still have the capacity for reatness.

Historical Heritage

Further Fallacies to Dehumanize African Americans

In my introduction, I have already discussed, briefly, the propaganda of some scholars who, had to formulate many destructive myths. These included myths that African American people have no historical, religion or cultural past in order to justify the barbaric act of enslaving Africans. The essence of these myths was to prove that the African American people have never made any contribution to World civilization. Overwhelmed with what we might call scholastic racism and pretense of simple ignorance, some of these scholars formulated the undocumented theory that Africans and African Americans have no history or civilization. Hegel, one of the greatest modern philosophers, in his lectures on the philosophy of history affirmed ignorantly that "Africa is no historical part of the world. It has neither movement nor development to exhibit.[13] Professor A.P. Newton and Hugh Trevor-Roper did not hesitate to formulate the theory that Africa (South of Egypt) had no history before its colonization by the Europeans.[14] David Hume, one of the greatest Scottish philosophers, said that he was suspicious of black people because they are neither animal nor human being, but form the link between the two.[15] Professor Arnold Toynbee also displayed the pretense of simple ignorance and scholastic racism when he maintained that there are twenty-one civilizations that have flourished in the world. "The Black Race has helped to create no civilization, while the Polynesian White Race has helped to create one civilization, the Brown Race two, the Yellow Race three, the Red Race and the Nordic White Race four apiece, the Alpin White Race nine, and the Mediterranean White Race, ten."[16] R. L. Johnstone reported the propagation of such myths during the early Colonial America:

> Early in Colonial American history the question arose
> concerning what to do about the religion of black slaves.
> One mandate said: Convert them to Christianity. But the
> other said: You shouldn't hold a fellow Christian as a
> slave. Therefore, what to do? Some slave owners quite
> expectedly opposed, the conversion of slaves. Uncon
> verted they presented no problem, since the slave owners
> would not be holding a fellow Christian as a slave. But
> theologians and clergymen said it was the Christian's

> obligation to teach the slaves Christianity and convert
> them. Some Southerners resolved the issue by defining
> blacks as less than human. We don't convert dogs, Ku
> dus, or zebras; therefore, we don't need to convert blacks
> as a lower animal form, they lack a soul to be saved.[17]

It suffices to name but a few of these scholars, since those few reputable scholars are enough to persuade you that it is not only ordinary men, but even some eminent scholars, that can be blindfolded with prejudice.

In the light of the above, it is vitally necessary that Africans and African-Americans study their history. Africans and African American scholars should publicize continuously the fact that Africans and African-Americans have rich historical, cultural and religious heritage. It is important that we emphasize the fact that modern historians, archaeologists, anthropologists and theologians have uncovered and have proved beyond any shadow of doubt that Africans and African-Americans have great historical, cultural and religious heritage, and that they have contributed immensely to the world civilization. Our purpose in this chapter is not to give elaborate historical details, but to mention in outline form some established facts about the history and the achievement of African Americans and their ancestors.

African American Ancestors' Contribution

African-American Ancestral Home As the Cradle of Mankind

During the early period of the study of the place of origin of mankind by the Western Scholars, the prevailing view is that Asia is the origin of the human race. Subsequent archaeological discovery did not support this theory, thus it becomes unsupportable by either historical or archaeological document. But modern discovery proved beyond any doubt that Africa is the cradle of the human race. Darwin, the Father of Natural Selection, says that it is more probable to locate the origin of mankind on the African continent than any other place in the world.[18] Dr. Albert Churchward, a distinguish medical man, anthropologist, archaeologist, and an outstanding member of both the Royal Council of Physicians and the Royal Council of Surgeons, maintained that the earliest man came from Great Lakes region of Africa from where they spread down the valley and settled in Egypt. From there, they later spread

Historical Heritage

to all parts of the world.[19]

Professor L. S. B. Leakey and his associates, who have been excavating in Africa for several years, did not hesitate to conclude that Africa is the birthplace of the human race. The fact is that the question of the origin of humankind has been settled.

African American Ancestors As The Originator of Civilization

Contrary to the previous opinion that Africans and Africa Americans have no history, informed modern scholars who are not blindfolded by scholastic racism have no hesitation in affirming the fact that the earliest civilization began in Africa. This modern view is in accord with biblical writers' opinion, which originated the civilization of Mesopotamia from the ancestors of African American people's home – Africans. In Genesis 10, Cush was the father of Nimrod, who built the Kingdom of Mesopotamia. If the word "Cush," both in biblical and modern Hebrew, has been used widely and specifically to refer to the home of the African-American ancestors (Africa) in the Egyptian and Assyrian records, it certainly refers to the African people in the biblical record. Therefore, the first builder of civilization in Mesopotamia was Nimrod, the son of Cush. This biblical tradition that civilization started by ancestors of African American people is in accord with the opinion of the Persians, the Greeks, and modern scholars.

African American Ancestors As the Inventor of the Art of Writing

We now have much evidence that the first writing system, called hieroglyphics, was invented in Africa. Even though some scholars agree that Africa is the cradle of the human race, they have found it absurd to accept the fact that the earliest system of writing originated from Africa, south of Egypt. They say that the Sumerians in Asia invented the earliest writing. However, the Egyptians' record (inscription of Hatshepshut) derived the origin of their writings from their Southern neighbors (Kushites and Puntites).[20] The Greek scholars1s unanimously maintained that African American forefathers (Africans) were the first of all men and that they were the most handsome, the tallest and the longest lived people of the world.

The fame of the Ethiopians was widespread in ancient history.

Historical Heritage

> Herodotus describes them as the tallest, most beautiful and long-lived of the human races, and before Herodotus, Homer, in even more flattering language described them as "the most just of men; the favorites of the gods." The annals of all the great early nations of Asia Minor are full of them. The Mosaic records allude to them frequently; but while they are described as the most powerful, the most just, and the most beautiful of human race, they are constantly spoken of as black, and there seems to be no other conclusion to be drawn than that at that remote period of history, the leading race of the Western World was a black race.[21]

Richard Lepsius, one of he finest German Egyptologist of great reputation was clear in his mind that the Nile Valley civilization was the oldest. He was certain that the early Sumerians imported that civilization including their writing from Africa. He said,

> In the oldest times within the memory of men we know of only one literary development, viz, those of Egypt, and we know of only one contemporary people which could have had knowledge of this culture, appropriated its results, and convey them to other nations, this was the Kushites, the masters of the Eurythraean Sea to its furthest limits. It was by them that Babylonia was colonized and fertilized with Egyptian culture. And it is thus only that the thoroughgoing correspondence between Babylonian knowledge and institutions and the Egyptian one becomes intelligible. The pictorial writing forming the basis of the cuneiform characters unmistakably only a species of the hieroglyphics; the astronomy of Babylon is only a development of that of Egypt; its unit of measure, that the royal architectural ell of 0.525, is completely identical with that of pyramids and obelisk, is an imperfect imitation of Egyptian originals and so with the other arts. At every step we meet in Babylonian with the trace of Egyptian models.[22]

The French orientalist, Count Constance Volney, after visiting Africa, was emphatic about Africa being the origin of civilization. He has this to say:

Historical Heritage

There is a people, now forgotten, discovered, while others were yet barbarious, the elements of art and sciences. A race of men now rejected from society for their sable skin and frizzed hair, founded or study of the laws of nature, those civic and religious systems which still govern the universe...I would be easy to multiply citation upon this subject; from all which follows, that we have the strongest reasons to believe that the country neighbouring to the tropic was the cradle of sciences, and consequence that the first learned nation was a nation of blacks; for it is incontrovertible, that by the term Ethiopians, the ancients
meant to represent a people of black complextion, thick lips and wooly hair.[23]

African American Ancestors As The Originator of Religion

Greek writers also maintained that Africans first originated of the worship of the gods. E. A. Wallis Budge, the distinguished antiquarian, Sir Henry Rawlinson, the Father of Assyriology (Assyrian), Richard Lepsius, one of the German Egyptologists (Egypt) of reputation, and others agreed that the art of writings and the worship of gods (Religion), originated from the home of the American ancestors.[24] In Sumer, all the gods and goddesses are children of "Anu," the king of the Sumerian gods and Professor Flinders Pretrie applies this term "Anu" or Annu to an original race of pre-dynastic Egypt.[25] That Africa is the origin of civilization has been maintained by several other scholars like Professor W. J. Perry of the University of Manchester, Count Constance Volney, the French Orientalist, and Dr. Ernest Albert Hooten, of the Department of Anthropology, Harvard University.[26]

African-American Ancestors As the Originator of Iron Smelting

Hooten, according to the result of his digging on the banks of Niger River in West Africa and Rhodesia, concluded that Africans were skilled iron workers for an indeterminate period.[27] Other scholars like Professor Franz Boas declared that the African American ancestors invented iron smelting while the Europeans were still using crude stone tools. These inventions have been very important for the advancement of human civilization.[28]

Historical Heritage

African American Ancestors Once Ruled the World

Between the tenth and seventh centuries B.C.E., several African rulers became protectors of Israel. As early as 700 B.C., King Hezekiah of Israel sent mission to Shabataka, the African King, instead of Assyrian King. When the Assyrians invaded Palestine, the children of Israel sent to the Africans for help. Shabataka sent military assistance arm in defense of Israel against the Assyrians. When the Assyrians threatened King Hezekiah of Judah, he depended upon the strength of the African King, Taharka. Sennacherib, the King of Assyria, launched his attack against Israel and the African King was later wiped out by a storm. Although the African kings was later defeated in their struggle to protect Israel, it is very significant that Israel cast their f ate on the Africans f or protection and the Africans did their best to protect Israel in the time of trouble **(II Kings 19:19; 11** Chronicle 12:3, 14:9, 12, 13). Around this period (eighth to seventh century B.C.E.), eyewitness account, archaeological and traditional material evidences show that the African American ancestors were in America even before Columbus ever dreamed of coming America. From this, it is very erroneous to say that all African American people were brought from Africa to America as slaves. More detailed evidences of the presence of African-American people before Columbus shall be given in the next section.

We learned that it was approximately during this period between (800-600 B.C.E.) that the African American ancestors dominated the entire known world of that day. They dominated Asia. His majesty, King Piankhi, ruled Africa, including Egypt and the entire World of that day. Piankhi left an inscription where he proclaimed himself the "Emperor of the World.[29] Honest historians often referred to his period as "an astonishing epoch of 'nigger' domination.[30] A respectable Egyptologist (Egypt), commenting on this claim of the African ruler, says that "It seems amazing that an African Negro should have been able with any sort of justification to style himself 'Emperor of the World.[31] Professor Weigall therefore has a chapter on this African ruler (Piankhi) which he titled, "The Exploits of a Nigger King.[32]

Historical Heritage

African American Ancestors in America Before Columbus Ever Dreamed of Coming to America

In the preceding sections, we have discussed the fact that African-American ancestors (Africans) were the first of the entire human race. They are the originator of civilizations, writings, religion, and iron smelting. I have also discussed the fact that there was a period when the African-American ancestors (Africans) ruled the entire known world, sometime between 800-600 B. C. E.

Several Americanists have claimed that the West has always been in the forefront in navigation, colonization and discoveries. They also assumed that Ancient America developed its cultures in isolation from the rest of the world until Columbus discovered America. We now know that Christopher Columbus never accepted such claim.[33]

Archaeological discovery, eyewitness accounts and Ancient American traditions supported the fact that during the period when the African-American ancestors ruled the entire World (800-600 B.C.E.), they were also in Ancient America. Further support for this claim will be forthcoming in the following discussion.

As early as the 3rd Millennium B.C.E., the African-American ancestors were sailing and trading with the Mesopotamian people. The Sumerians referred to these African people as Magan and Meluhha. The Sumerians traded in wood, gold and other precious materials. If the African American ancestors could sail to Mesopotamia, there should be no question of whether they could have reached Ancient America. We have several evidences that before Christopher Columbus ever dreamed of coming to America, the African American ancestors were already in America.[34]

When Professor Leakey, an outstanding archaeologist, who has dug extensively in Africa, was asked whether he thinks that Africans migrated to America, he replied, It is inconceivable that man, the most curious and mobile animals, would not have come to America when the elephants, the tapirs and deer came from Asia ... man spread out from Asia to Europe. It is inconceivable that he would stay out of America .... At least people should go look for remains of man before they say he wasn't in America" (Jeanne Reinert, "The Man Dr. Leakey Dug Up,"

Science Digest, vol. 60, no. 5, Nov. 1966)

The claim by scholars who are bent on debasing African American people that African people could not have been able to sail so far to Ancient America so early and that all African American people came as slaves has no foundation. It should be discarded.

In addition to the paintings on the walls of temples and tombs, and the evidence of an ancient shipwreck, the oldest preserved vessel in the world was discovered in the home of the African American ancestors (Africa) in *1954*. This was the magnificent papyrus boat of Cheops built around *2,600* B.C.E., which is *1461/2* feet long and almost *20* feet wide" When there was a dispute as to whether this type of boat made with papyrus could ever sail across the Atlantic Ocean, such boats were put into a series of tests. According to Sertima[35] Thor Heyerdahl, a Norwegian writer and explorer, organized the building of papyrus boats like that of Cheops f found at Gizah. After the completion of the papyrus boats, built by Africans, he named the boat RA I, and set sail from Africa to the Atlantic to America on May *25, 1969*. As the RA I boat approached Barbados, it got into trouble mainly because of the mistake made by the builder of the boat. The removal of the rope which "acted as a spring supporting the pliant afterdecck in the Egyptian model caused RA I to sag and it could not complete the journey. Another boat call RA II, identical to the Egyptian boat, was built by the Aymara tribe (native American tribe). Having learned from the error of RA 1, they sailed successfully across the Atlantic from Africa to America.

Apart from the above practical proof that Ancient Africans were capable of sailing across the Atlantic to America, we have record that the African King of the Third Dynasty (Pharaoh Sneferu) made approximately sixty ships that were about 100 feet long. In the following year we were told that he built three more ships "with a bow -to-stern measurement of about 170 feet.

We also have records of a ship of the Egyptians and of the Ethiopians in the Sumerian inscriptions as early as the third millennium B.C.E. During the time of Naran-Sin and Gudea of Lagash, Egypt and Ethiopia were called Magan and Meluhha.[36] African-American ancestors traded with the Sumerians in gold, timber and all kinds of precious stones. The Sumerians captured some of the African ships. The above evidence make it reasonably certain that African American ancestors from Africa have been masters of the sea from time immemorial and were able to sail to every part of the ancient known World. It was therefore not impossible for Africans to sail to America for colonization or trade before Columbus, as some maintain.

Eyewitness Testimonies Concerning African American Ancestors' Discovery of America

African Secret Route to America

When Christopher Columbus was in Portugal, King Don Juan of Portugal told Columbus that Africans in Guinea reported to him saying that they had set out from Guinea, West Africa with merchandise for sale, through some secret route to America. [37]

Africans Traded in Gold and Spears with Native Americans

Although Christopher Columbus could not find the African secret route to America, what the Indians at Haiti and the Dominican Republic (Espaniola) told him was a confirmation of that route. These Indians told Columbus that they were already trading in gold and iron with Africans. As a proof, they brought to Columbus some African spears whose tops were made of metal called gua-nin.[38] When Columbus sent the samples of these African spears to the King of Portugal, he discovered that "of 32 parts, 18 were of gold, 6 of silver, and 8 of copper." The origin of the word guanin was traced to the Mande languages of West Africa by Sertima; that is, "through Mandingo, Karíbunga, Toronka, Kankanke, Bambara, Mande and Vei."[39] When Christopher Columbus was in Cape Verde, he found other confirmation of King Juan's secret route from Africa to America. He was told that the African American ancestors "had been known to set out to the Atlantic from the Guinea coast of Africa in canoes loaded with merchandise and going toward the West.[40]

African Handkerchiefs Found in America

The report by Africans above influenced Columbus' third voyage. When he arrived in one of the Caribbean Islands, he named that Island Trinidad (1498) because of the three rocks he found there which reminded him of the Trinity.[41] On August 7, 1498 when Columbus arrived in South America, the natives brought some cotton handkerchiefs very symmetrically woven and colourful, exactly like those brought from African Guinea. These cotton handkerchiefs were not only similar in style and color, they were functioned for headdresses and loin clothes.[42]

The Spanish Explorer Vaco Munez Balboa in 1513 Saw Africans in America

When Balboa arrived in an Indian settlement near Quarequa, he saw many "Black" people among the Indians who were war captives. These were unmistakably "Africans." Balboa was so astonished to see these tall and strong African men of war that he asked the Indians from where they got these Black men. The Indians answered Balboa that they did not know the origin of those men, except that men of that color (Black) "were living nearby and they were constantly waging war against them.[43] Peter Martyr, who is regarded as the first historian of America, describes these Africans at Darien:

> The Spaniards . . . found Negroes in this province. They only live one day's march from Quaregua and they are fierce. ... It is thought that Negro pirates from Ethiopia established themselves after the wreck of their ships in these mountains. The natives of Quaregua carry on an incessant war with these Negroes. Massacre or slavery is the alternate fortune of these peoples.[44]

This encounter is the first actual encounter with the African men in the Indies and the word slaves does not in any way signify the buying of slaves from Africa or confirm a view that African people wherever they were found were slaves, as some scholars maintain.
These were examples of inter-tribal wars common in those regions where captives were molested and punished, as the Indians indicated. The Black tribes' also took some of these Indians captives. Balboa also met "a group of seventeen Africans shipwrecked in Ecuador in the early sixteenth century among whom later became the governors of an entire province of American Indians."[45]

Historical Heritage

Amerigo Vespucci's Testimony

Vespucci, during his journey to the Carribbean Island called Curacao Osland of Giants), mentioned some strange race of men who were extraordinarily tall. These men and women who were described as giants were "as a head and a half" (or a foot and a half) taller than any of the Spaniards there. Frederick Poffi, Vespucci's distinguished biographer, holds the opinion that these giants were Black men.[46] I think that Frederick is right when we consider other descriptions of Africans in antiquity. The Hebrew records regard the Africans as very powerful and tall men (Isaiah 18:1-6, 20:1-6). The classical Greeks considered Africans as the most handsome and the tallest men on earth.[47]

African-American Ancestors Took Part in the Spanish Exploration to America 1528-1530

It is a known fact that we had Africans participating in some of the earliest explorations by the Spanish people to America. Estevaníco (Little Stephen) was with Cabeza de Vaca during his years of wandering from Florida to Mexico (1528-1530). Also in 1539, Estevanico, as a guide to the Miza Expedition, went out with Fríar Marcos de Miza from Mexico in search of the fabled "Seven Cities of Cibola." When other people in this company wearied, Estevanico continued alone, except for the Indian guides. As a result, what is now known as Arizona and New Mexico were opened to the European settlers.

Testimonies by Early Missionaries About African Tribes that Were in America Before Columbus

It is interesting that the evidence supporting the presence of African people in America before Columbus is not limited to the Spanish and Portuguese explorers. When Rev. Father Roman, one of the earliest Catholic missionaries arrived in the New World, he reported about the presence of the tribe of Black men" who came from the South armed to the teeth with darts of guanin (gold spears) and landed in Haiti. These men were referred to as 'Black Guaninis." Referring to these Black men, Peter Dario says:

Historical Heritage

These might have been the Negroes of Quareca, mentioned by Peter Martyr d'Anglena, or some other American Negro nation - the like of which there were many, as we may see in Rafinesque's *"Account of the Ancient Black Nations of America."* Such are the Charruas of Brazil, the Black (arabees of St. Vincent), in the Gulf of Mexico, the Jamassi of Florida, the dark complexioned Californians who are perhaps the dark men mentioned in the Quiche traditions and some old Spanish adventures. Such, again, is the tribe of which Balboa saw some representatives in his passage of the Isthrnus of Darian in the year *1513*[48]

Another early missionary, Fray Gregoria Garcia, "a priest of the Dominican order" who spent about nine years in Peru *(1500 C.E.)*, reported that it was in the Island of Cartagena, Colombia, where the Spanish people first encountered the Black people in the Americas.'

Another eyewitness testimony we have is a recent observation of a modern writer, Colonel Braghine, who visited the equatorial forest of French Guiana, in the 1940's. There he saw a local Negro tribe of Saramaccas, who were living and ruling themselves. Their administrative system involves division into clans, each with its coat of arms tattooed on the faces of the members. Braghine himself files the following report of his visit:

> Once I had the opportunity of living for about a month in Oyapoc, a locality in a lonely situation among the equatorial forest of French Guiana. There I saw representatives of the local Negro tribe of Saramaccas, which five all by itself and is ruled by its own chiefs. The Saramaccas are divided into several clans and each clan possesses a sort of coat of arms tattoed on the faces of its members . . . . The Sararnacca tongue resembles the dialect of the African Gold Coast, which is situated directly opposite the Guianna shores. I am inclined to believe that the Saramaccas are the last Aboriginal Negro tribe preserved in America.[49]

Some scholars regard these "Black" people to be the African people brought here by slavery, but such does not make sense in this situation. First, it is improbable that a whole tribe would be transported as slaves.

Historical Heritage

Second, even if a whole tribe is transported, it is improbable that all could escape from their masters to form unblemished black tribes as some have maintained. So we may accept Braghine's view that they were African people who came to America during the pre-Columbus days.[50]

The above discussion of the eyewitness account of the presence of African American Ancestors before Columbus is a few of the evidences available. Others include some strong archaeological evidences, and Indian and African traditions to which we shall now turn.

Archaeological Evidence of African Presence in America Before Columbus

Scholars unanimously agree that using archaeological materials to reconstruct the history of a particular people is a delicate issue because material remains that are uncovered have to be interpreted. At times, the interpretation of these materials is subject to the prejudices and bias of the interpreters. Yet, no informed scholar would deny the fact that the use of these archaeological remains to reconstruct a history of a particular people has produced great results in the field of productive scholarship. This is particularly true in the case of the history of the people of the ancient Near East (Egypt, Israel, Assyria, Persia, Sumer, etc.) In the case of the history of the African people and their pre-Columbus presence in Americas, the result of archaeological remains cannot be overestimated. It is so overwhelming that it cannot be ignored.

Stone Heads in Vera Cruz

The first and the most important archaeological evidence is the discovery in Mexico of huge stone heads with African characteristics. The first of these stone heads that we know of was found in the jungle of Vera Cruz by several archaeological parties. This stone head (called cabeza colossal by the Mexicans) was first spotted by J. M. Melgar, who noticed the African characteristics and then brought it to the attention of the public in 1869. This information reached Dr. Matthew W. Stirling, the then Director of the Bureau of American Ethnology of the Smithsonian Institution, Washington, D. C. After visiting Vera Cruz, Dr. Stirling organized an expedition, sponsored jointly by the Smithsonian Institution and the National Geographic Society, to unearth the African head near the

Historical Heritage

village of Tres Zapatos. The stone head was six feet high, and eighteen feet in circumference, and it weighed over ten tons. The African head was wearing a helmet. Near this location was also found some steel with dots and crosses which yielded a date - November 4, 291 B.C.E." This date indicates that Black people have been present in America as early as 291 B. C. E. When there was a doubt concerning the dating (291 B. C. E.) modern scientific dating system (Carbon 14) was applied to another remain in that area; the result was the same.[51]

Stone Heads in La Venta

In 1939, Dr. Stirling made an expedition to another location called La Venta near the coast of the Gulf of Mexico, and dug out a second stone head. This second stone head was first seen and photographed by the University of Tulane Expedition in 1925. When Dr. Stirling saw this picture, he was surprised to see that this head resembled the head he had excavated at Vera Cruz near Zapatos. He went to La Venta in 1939 with his group and excavated another stone head, eight feet high, with African characteristics (thick lips and broad nose) like the former excavated in Vera Cruz. Three more gigantic African heads were excavated at La Venta. Two of these heads were extraordinarily realistic in details. Ivan Van Sertima described this detail in a very vivid way:

The lines of cheek and jaw, the fullness of the lips, the broadly fleshed nose, the acutely observed and faithfully reproduced facial contour and particulars bore eloquent witness to a Negro-African presence. One of the Negroid Colossi, eight and half feet high in circumference, wore ear plugs with a cross carved in cache. They all wore headdresses that were foreign and distinctive - domed helmets like those of ancient soldiers. They all faced east, starting at the Atlantic.[52]

When the modern scientific dating (Carbon 14) was applied, the result was astonishing. Carbon 14 dating yielded a date not later than 814 B. C. E.[53] Most Americanists accept 800 B. C. E. as the earliest date for the La Venta site.

When we matched this date with the events in Africa, the result or the implication is interesting. The period between 985 to about 400 B. C. E. is known as the period when the Africans south of Egypt dominated Egypt and the known ancient world. One period of particular interest is the period of Piankhi. Several Egyptologists referred to his period as the period of "Nigger domination." From this, it is very possible that African people extended their influence to America by trading and dominating the people. This happens to be the very period when the Olmec culture flourished in South America.

Other African Stone Heads

The above mentioned African heads in Tres Zapatos and La Venta are by no means the only African heads uncovered in America. Five more Negroid heads were uncovered at San Lorenzo, southeast of Vera Cruz in 1967, by the group led by Dr. Michael Coe of Yale University. These remains excavated by Stirling, Coe and other archaeologists belong to the Olmec culture.

Other African stone heads were found in the Temple of Danzantes. There were also several "relief figures on large stone slab. Most of these over forty figures were Africans. Some seem to be dancing or swimming.[54]

Some other remarkable archaeological evidence includes the realistic portrait of Africans in clay, gold and stone unearthed in pre-Columbian strata in Central and South America."[55] The practice of mummification, which was prevalent in Africa, was also found in Ancient Mexico. "One of the best examples of this is the mummies in the sarcophagus at Palenque, with jade masks on their faces and the flared base of the sarcophagus." These features remain as further evidence of the American and African contact in the pre-Columbian America. This evidence of mummification is not limited to South and Central America, it is a practice widespread in North America. It was found among the "Indian tribes of Virginia, North Carolina, and Congarees of South Carolina and those of Florida.[56]

Of great importance is the fact that Amerindians venerated African gods. Among the Maya and Aztecs, African portraits were worshipped as deities. Colonel Bragbine attests to these African figures: "Some statues of the Indian gods in Central America possess typical Negro features and certain prehistoric statues there undoubtedly represent Africans. We have, for instance, such statues in Teotihaucan, in Palenque, a gigantic African head carved in granite near the Mexican volcano Tatila' . The Mexican historian Riva-Palacio was quoted as saying: "It is indisputable that in very ancient times the Negro race occupied our territory (Mexico) . The Mexicans recall a Negro god, Ixtilton which means black-face.[57]

Historical Heritage

Speaking about the African influence on the Mayan religious culture before Columbus, A. H. Verrill, of the Museum of the American Indian, New York, who has a thorough knowledge of the customs and languages of the Indians of Latin America, says: "Even today, many of the Indians of Central and South America secretly venerate or worship the gods of their forefathers. The Mayan tribes are no exception, although of ten the ancient Mayan deities and rites and Christian rituals and saints are almost inextricably confused."[58]

In the little church of Esquipultas, Guatemala, is the image of the Black Christ to which thousands of Indians journey annually from all parts of Central America and even from Mexico and South America. Moreover, among many of the *Indians* the Black Christ is referred to in private as Ekchuah or as Hunabku (the former, the Mayan god of merchants, husbandmen, and travellers; the latter, the *God-father* or supreme deity of the Mayas), of ten prefixed with the Spanish Cristo (Christ), as Cristo Ekchuah or as Cristo Hunabku.[59]

Amerindian Tradition

The fact that tradition is treated as the last evidence for the pre-Columbian presence of the African-American ancestors in America before Columbus, by no means suggests that tradition, written or oral, is less important. In fact, oral tradition among the ancient people is the most important vehicle of communication and instruction. This is especially true among the people of the ancient Near East and also among the ancient Amerindian. Nicholas Leon, who is considered one of the eminent Mexican authorities, tells us about Amerindian oral traditions.[60] According to him, one of the native American traditions holds that "the oldest inhabitants of Mexico were Negroes." He further says:

> Nearly all the races of our soil commonly believe the existence of Negro and giants and in their various languages they had words to designate them. Several archaeological objects found in various localities demonstrate their existence, the most notable of which is the colossal granite head of Hueyapan, Vera Cruz, and an axe of the same located near the city. In Teotihua abound little heads of the Ethiopian type and paintings of African-American ancestors, In Michaocan and Oxaca the same have been found.[61]

Historical Heritage

The pre-Columbian blacks which the Mongoloid Americans referred to, and enshrined in their oral traditions, were certainly not themselves, but "an unusual outsider-, in most cases an object of mystery and reverence, and, moreover, a figure who began to feature prominently in their world in historic time (that is, from the Olmec civilization onward). Here, it is important to note that the references to giants correspond to Amerigo Vespucci's strange race of "tall men sighted on a Caribbean Island," which Frederick Pohl (Vespucci's biographer), believes were "black men." This reference to giants in the Amerindian tradition also corresponds with Herodotus' (Father of History) description of the Africans as the tallest men in the world (*Herodotus*, Bk. D.

Again, Jairazbhoy mentions an oral tradition among the Amerindian, which was recorded in Popul Vuh (Bible of Quiche Maya), which appears to indicate the place from where these "Blacks" came by ships. This tradition seems to indicate that they were blown off course into the North Atlantic current and landed at Panuco in "seven wooden ships or galleys."[62] This same tradition also refers to "black people, pale-skinned people who came to their land from the land of the sunrise."[63]

In the light of the foregoing evidence of the pre-Columbian presence of African Americans, one wonders upon what basis Columbus is hailed as the discoverer of America. What may appear to be the reason is lack of adequate knowledge of the African American ancestors. If so, then now that this evidence is available to the public, there should be a re-examination of such false historical information in the name of objective scholarship. It is important to re-examine and reverse this idea of Columbian discovery of America, so as not to continue to mislead the public.

It is also appropriate to ask the question on what basis is the myth of the innate inferiority of the people called "Black" propounded by some scholars? Why will Olmec civilization erect huge monuments to him, if they were inferior beings? Why will they be venerated if the Negroes were beasts and irresponsible people? Why would they (Negroes) be venerated if they were nothing but beggars "in the wilderness of history," "porters," "peddlers," "mercenaries" and "eternal and immutable" slaves before and after Columbus?[64] How can the idea of independent African culture before Arab and Roman gold-trade be pure "nonsense," when the Spanish explorers and missionaries reported the presence of African-American ancestors in America when they first arrived? How can the Negro-American simply be conducting the "Islamic cultural electricity" when the Amerindian tradition regards African people as the original inhabitants of Mexico? There would be too many contradictions for such ideas to be true. It is, of course, contrary to common sense for such to be. It is time to change the myth that Africans and African-Americans are eternally inferior.

African American Ancestors Built Well-Organized and Powerful Empires Before the Arrival of the Slavers and Colonizers.

Contrary to all the misconceptions that the ancestors of African Americans had no civilization and no history before the coming of the colonizers and enslavers, there is abundant evidence that they had built powerful, well-organized States before the coming of the kidnappers, who stole and forced Africans to come to the U. S. and other parts of the world. Ghana, Songhay, Mafi, and Kanem-Bornu Empires were established in West Africa as early as 700 C.E. Before the coming of the destroyers, the African-American ancestors in Africa, "lived in a society where university life was fairly common and scholars were beheld with reverence." As early as the sixteenth century C.E., the City of Timbuktu in the Songhay Empire, West Africa, had become the intellectual center of Africa. In Timbuktu was established "The University of Sankore."[65] The University of Sankore enjoyed a great prestige in higher education under the reign of Askia the Great of the Songhay Empire. The University professors visited other universities in Morocco, Egypt and Spain. Professor Mohammed Abu Bekr of Sankore was one of its outstanding professors of the sixteenth century C.E. Another outstanding scholar, formerly a student of Mohammed Abu Bekr, was Ahmed Baba. He was the last chancellor of the University of Sankore and authored about forty books before the City of Timbuktu was invaded, the citizens of Timbuktu rounded up, and deported to Morocco on March 18, 1594.[66] When Professor Ahmed Baba protested against this invasion, he was imprisoned and later exiled to Morocco. During his exile to Morocco, his collection of 1,600 volumes of books were l0st.71 The above is enough to discount the fallacious belief that the Africans and African-Americans have no history, no culture, no civilization and no heritage of any kind. It is very important for all African American people, old and young, to know this

Historical Heritage

important fact and be proud of their heritage. Therefore, no African and African American should rest until every African-American in the United States and elsewhere knows this historical heritage.

If the African American ancestors were the origin of the human race, the origin of civilization, and the builders of powerful kingdoms and as a result were held very highly in esteem, why are Africans in the situation they are now? What is responsible for the destruction the answer to these questions is the task of the next section, where the institution of slavery will be discussed.

As part of the answer to these questions, there is a need to ask where the civilizations of the Sumerians, the Hittites, the Assyrians, the Babylonians, the Persians, and the Romans, and probably "the Great Britain" today? They have gone into the drain. This is because as history reveals that "what comes into being goes out of being." African ancient civilizations became part of that essence of history, which came to being and went out of being. However, something make that of Africa appear worse. The present decline is not caused by Africans hating themselves, but by the European and American rape of African of its human and God-given natural resources.

The Rape of African American Ancestors' Land

You may wonder the reason I chose to discuss the history of the inhuman institution of slavery when African-American people are trying to forget such a bitter experience. Apart from the fact that it is part of the history of the African Americans, it is important to know this history in order to disprove further fallacies of the slaveholders. In an attempt to rip the African Americans of their identity, they were taught that other Africans hated them and that was the reason why the Africans sold them out to the enslavers. Although it is clearly known that Africans did not bring any of their brothers or sisters across the sea (but the enslavers went across the sea to Africa), they still maintain the fallacy that their African ancestors sold them. In this light, it is very important to discuss briefly how slavery began, and describe the method of obtaining slaves.

The Beginning of the Rape
of African-American Ancestors

The institution of slavery destroyed the great achievements of Africa. The opening up of America to the Europeans and the expansionistic and imperialistic ambition of the Europeans in the fifteenth century was responsible for the establishment of the institution of slavery. Underlying this expansionism, was the search for new markets, materials, new manpower and new land to exploit.[67]

As early as 1441-1442, Antonio Gonsalvez and Nuno Tristan went to the Sahara Coast of Africa and while coming back brought back gold dust and ten black slaves. When these slaves were sent to Pope Martin V, he conferred upon Portugal the possession and sovereignty over all countries to be discovered from Cape Blanco in Africa to India.[68] The devilish and barbarous slave business increased when the natives of Peru and Mexico were forced to slavery in mines and "their death rate was so high" that their European masters were forced to look somewhere else for slave labor. We were told that it was the honorable Bishop of Chiapa who gave them the direction of Africa in 1517 by proposing that each Spanish gentleman be allowed to import twelve African slaves.[69] The result was that 4000 slaves were imported annually from Africa to Cuba, Hispaniola, Jamaica and Puerto Rico. Following this, nearly all the nations of Europe were involved in this uncivilized and inhuman business.

John Hawkins was the first prominent Englishman to engage in slavery. The slave ship used for this slave trade was named Jesus and belonged to Queen Elizabeth.[70] The Rev. John Newton, the Rector of St. Mary Woolroth, London, the writer of the song "How *Sweet the Name of Jesus*, spent his youthful years as the commander of a slave ship in Gold Coast (Ghana).

Method of Obtaining Slaves in Africa

The method of capturing the Africans is the worst human treatment in history. These methods include burning of towns, robbery or stealing, spreading terror and detribalizing the African natives. When they first arrived in Africa in 1498, they pretended they were bringers of good tidings. The Kings and their people were very friendly, because Africans by nature are friendly to strangers. However, as *Kilwa Chronicle* describes it ". . . those who knew the truth confirmed that they were corrupt and dishonest persons who had only come to spy out the land in order to seize it.

Lest I am accused of inventing lies against the race of people to

Historical Heritage

whom I owe my education, I will quote extensively to support such brutal and devilish methods of kidnapping Africans and bringing them to the New World. Let us begin with an eyewitness record. Hans Mayr, who was on board one of the slave ships to Mozambique, gives this description of the nefarious event:

> As soon as the town had been taken without opposition, the Vicar-General and some of the Franciscan fathers came ashore carrying two crosses in their possession and singing the *Te Deum*. They went to the palace, and there the cross was put down and the Ground Captain prayed. Then everyone started to plunder the town of all its merchandise and provisions. . . .The Grand-Captain ordered that the town should be sacked and that each man should carry off to his ship whatever he found: So that at the end there would be a division of the spoil, each man to receive a twentieth of what he found. The same rule was made for gold, silver and pearls. Then everyone started to plunder the town and search the houses forcing open the doors with axes and iron bars. There was a large quantity of cotton cloth for sofala in the town, for the whole coast gets its cotton from here . . . . A large quantity of rich silk and gold embroidered clothes was seized and carpet also; one of these, which was without equal for beauty, was sent to the King of Portugal together with many other valuables.[71]

Professor Emil Torday, during his lecture in Geneva in 1931 under auspices of the Society for the Protection of Children of Africa is quoted as saying that:

> The slavers scoured the Guinea Coast, not being contented with the devastation of one area. As they devastated an area they moved westward and then southward, spreading confusion, anarchy, and ruin wherever they went. They extended the gospel of doom past the Niger, down to the Congo Basin, past Luango and Angolar, down South to the Cape of Good Hope, and by 1789, they had initiated Mozambique into their slave-raiding ideology. They manufactured quarrels among tribesmen and set them at each other's throats, taking care, of course, to supply them weapons. The propagandists and the religious hypocrites of

the time claimed that however cruel was the traffic in human flesh, the African slave in the West Indies and in America was happier than in his own country.[72]

An eminent Africanist gave another accurate description of this evil act:

> From the black men digging in the fields about the village, a cry of sudden fear went up. Women shrieked and children scurried for hiding as if pursued by lions .... then all the men, in terror dashed into their huts, seized spears, and any other weapons they could grab, and, herding their families into the shelter of the surrounding forest, swore by all the tribal gods to sell themselves dearly. . . .They knew that other Africans, multitudes of them, had been captured, that villages had been left desolate and empty; that children had been orphaned, mothers wrested from their sons, sons from their mothers, husbands from their wives; and that lives of whole communities had been devastated as by volcanic blasts. For these strangers from across the waters were pitiless hunters - hunters of men.[73]

Edmund B. D'Avergne describes how these enslavers hunted people as hunters hunt foxes and deer in the forest:

> Hunting people often say they hunt the fox and deer in order to save these poor animals from being exterminated by the cruel farmers. Dom Henry's motive for kidnapping black folks at the estuaries of the Senegal and Gambia may have been similarly unselfish.[74]

Even when there was a decree to abolish slave trade, the rape of Africa continued. They colonized Africa and claimed her products. During colonization in Africa, King Leopold of Belgium issued a decree to neglect nothing in "exploiting the forest" in Congo. Lord Russell graphically described this method of exploiting the Africans:

> Each village was ordered by the authorities to collect and bring in a certain amount of rubber - as much as the men could bring in by neglecting all work for their own maintenance. If they

failed to bring the required amount, their women were taken away and kept as hostages in compounds or in the harems of government employees. If this method failed, native troops, many of them cannibals, were sent into villages to spread terror, if necessary, by killing some of the men; but in order to prevent a waste of cartridges they were ordered to bring one right hand for every cartridge used. If they missed, or used cartridges on game, they cut off the hands on living persons to make up the necessary number. The result was, according to the estimate of Sir H. H. Johnson, which is confirmed from all other impartial sources, that in fifteen years the native population was reduced from about twenty million to scarcely nine million.[75]

Experience of the African-American Ancestors on the Passage between Africa and America

The pain and suffering endured by these Africans seem to be beyond description. When they got into the ship, the torture was definitely not less from, the process of their capture. It was during their journey from West Africa to America and the West Indies that their anguish reached its peak. They were forced to crowd into canoes by whips and spears before reaching the ship. They were packed on one another like sardines. Although the women were not chained, the men were chained in pairs, "ankle to ankle," and "wrist to wrist." When asked how comfortable were the slaves, the Captain of the ship replied, "They are about as comfortable as a man might be in his coffin."[76]

The Physician who was on board of the slave ships had a better description of what his eyes beheld during the middle passage:

> Some wet and blowing weather having occasioned the port-holes to be shut and the grating to be covered, fluxes and fevers among the Negroes resulted. While they were in this situation, my profession requiring it, I frequently went down among them, till at length their apartments became so extremely hot as to only sufferable for a very short time. But the excessive heat was not the ~only thing that rendered their situation intolerable. The deck, that is, the floor of their rooms, was so covered with the blood and mucus, which had proceeded from them in consequence of the flux, that it resembled a slaughterhouse. It is

Historical Heritage

not in the power of the human imagination to picture a situation more dreadful and disgusting. Numbers of the slaves had fainted; they were carried on deck, where several of them died, and the rest were with difficulty restored. It nearly proved fatal to me also.[77]

In 1781, a case was brought to the English Court, not because of murdering, but of insurance. A slave ship of 442 slaves was so crowded that sixty of them died and another ninety Africans were thrown overboard. Thirty-six more were drowned because of lack of water" During another trip from West Africa, no fewer than 2,053 died out of 7,904 [78] slaves shipped. Only God knows how many African slaves died during the middle passage. All we can do is to imagine them. David Livingston describes that "one slave in three was killed in raids or on the trip to the Coast," and out of three human cargoes on the voyage across the sea, one sank. All in total, not less than 100,000,000 African Negroes died as a result of the slave trade' By 1576, about 40,000 African slaves were in Latin America. By 1800, this number had increased to 776,000. In 1767 in Jamaica, there were 140,000 slaves, but by 1800, the number rose to 300,000. In Virginia by 1620 a group of 20 slaves were imported, but by 1760, it rose to 200,000. It was believed that the total number of African slaves imported to the English Colonies of America and West Indies was about 40,000,000.[79]

The Arrival of African American Ancestors in America

Despite all sacrifices to the gods for deliverance from pain, the inhuman and barbarous business continued. Africans could not understand what on earth they had done against the gods of the land to allow them to go through such horror. As if such horror, pain and anguish during captivity at home and on the way to America were not enough, when they arrived at the New World, they had to endure the process of examination by their purchasers. C. R. James aptly described the experience of those who survived the terrible and deadly journey:

> When the ship reached the harbour, the cargo came up on deck to be bought. Their purchasers examined them for defects, looked at the teeth, pinched the skin, sometimes tasted the perspirations to see if the slave's blood was pure and the health

Historical Heritage

as good as his appearance. Some of the women affected curiosity, the indulgence of which, with a horse, would have caused them to be kicked twenty yards across the deck. But the slaves had to stand it. Then in order to restore dignity which might have been lost by too intimate an examination, the purchasers spat on the face of the slaves. Having become the property of his owner, he was branded on both sides of the breast with a hot iron. His duties were explained by an interpreter and a priest instructed him in the first principles of Christianity."[80]

The Official Chronicler of Portugal, Eannes de Azurara, described another vivid description of the state of the first large confinement of the African slaves,

> On the eighth day of August 7, 1444, very early in the morning on account of the heat, the mariners began to assemble their lighters and to disembark their captives, according to their orders. Which captives were gathered together in a field, and marvelous it was to see among them some of the rosy whiteness, fair and well-made; others less white, verging on grey; other again as black as moles, as various in their complexions as in their shapes, . . . and what heart was so hard as not to be moved to pity by the sight of this multitude, some with bowed heads and tearful countenances, when groaning deliriously and with eyes uplifted toward the heavens, as if to implore help from the Father of all mankind; while there were others who covered their faces with their hands and flung vent to their sorrow in a dirge, after the manner of their country; and although we could not understand the words, well, we appreciated the depth of their distress. And now to aggravate their woe; men came to parcel them out into five distinct lots, to do which they tore the son from his father, the wife from the husband, one brother from his brethren. No tie of blood and comradeship respected; each was thrown into a place by chance. O irresistible fortune, thou which ridest roughshod over the affairs of this world, bring to the knowledge of these most unhappy folk those ultimate truths from which they may receive consolation And ye that are charged with this division into lots, deplore so great a misery, and observe how these unhappy ones embrace one another so

tightly that it needs no little strength to tear them apart. Such division indeed, was not to be effected without great trouble; since parents and children, finding themselves in different groups, would run back to each other - mothers clutched up their children and ran away with them, caring not about the blows they received so long as their little ones should not be torn from them. After this toilsome fashion was the task of division accomplished, the work being rendered more difficult by the crowds, which flocked from the neighboring towns and villages, neglecting their work, to see this novel sight. And some of these spectators moved to tears, others chattering, they made tumult, which hindered those charged with business. The Infante (Dom Henry) mounted on a powerful horse, disdained to take his own share, some forty-six souls, but threw back into common stock, taking pleasure only in thought of so many souls being redeemed from perdition. And truly, his hope was not in vain, since so soon as they learned the language, with very little trouble, these people became Christians, and I who write this history saw afterward in the town of Lagos,9 young men and women, the offspring of these, born in the Country, good and genuine Christians as if they had been descended from the generation first baptized under the dispensation of Christ.[81]

Such was the fate of the African American ancestors under the slavers' pretense of Christianizing the African American ancestors.

At this point, the questions that may be appropriately asked are: Where was the Church when this evil was going on? What part did the Church play? The answers to those questions are not difficult to find. Some of these answers have been provided in the preceding discussion, but more elaboration shall be done below.

Although the Church later participated in the movement of abolition of slavery, they are not exempted from the havoc that had already been done through their participation in the inhuman business. As stated earlier, at the beginning of slavery in 1441 when ten African-American ancestors were sent to Pope Martin V, the honorable Pope first conferred upon Portugal the right of possession and sovereignty all over the land that might be "discovered" from Africa to India.[82] This was done, because the Pope reasoned that the heathens had no heritage on earth. As early as 1517 when the enslavers discovered that the people of Peru and Mexico could not endure the torture of slavery because their death rate was so high, it was Bartolome de las Casas, the Bishop of Chiapa who directed the people of Spain to Africa.[83]

John Hawkins, the first notable English slaver of importance, was described as a pious man" who admonished his sailors to "Serve God daily," and named his slave ship Jesus. Nevertheless, he proceeded to kidnap men of Cape Verde in Africa. When he reached Latin America,, he compelled the settlers to buy slaves at his own price.

When the towns of Kilwa and Mombasa were sacked, without any opposition, we are told that the Vicar-General and some Franciscan Fathers came ashore, prayed and began to plunder the town of all its merchandise and provisions. Again, we have this record from the pen of a slave raider himself:

And at length Our Lord God, who rewarded all that is well done, ordained that in return for the work of this day done by our men in this service they should have the victory and the reward of their fatigues and disbursements in the taking of one hundred and sixty-five captives, men, women and children, without recording those that died or that killed themselves."[84]

As late as the nineteenth century, the Reverend James Wilson regarded slavery as "That gracious and benevolent system which elevates the heathen cannibal into the contented civilized, intelligent domestics we see around us. Nay, more, into humble, faithful and most joyous worshippers of the true and everlasting God. Bless God for such a system. We don't apologize for slavery, we glory in it, and no society shall exist within our border that disqualifies or stigmatizes the slave trade.[85]

We also recall an incident of a slave raid on Sunday on the West African Coast. When the Captain of the ship found out that these captives were captured on Sunday, they turned back their ship to shore. The African captives were turned loose and then recaptured on the weekdays to avoid the desecration of the Sabbath day.[86] It is very unfortunate that despite all the protests, and the opposition of Pope Pius II (fifteenth century), Pope Paul III (in the sixteenth century), Pope Urban VIII (seventeenth century), and Pope Benedict (eighteenth century), both Catholic and Protestants ignored and continued more than ever this devilish work. Among men who also protested against slavery and stood firm for Christianity were the Quakers, John Wesley, Professor Adam Smith and Dr. Samuel Johnson. But all of this was to no avail until a later time through the effort

Historical Heritage

of Granville Sharp and William Wilberforce.

In the early colonial days in America, the American divines had problems deciding whether the Black slaves from Africa had souls or not. I will quote again the words of Ronald Johnstone:

> Early in colonial American history the question arose concerning what to do about the religion of black slaves. One mandate said: Convert them to Christianity. But the other said: You shouldn't hold a fellow Christian as a slave. Therefore, what to do? Some slave owners quite expectedly opposed the conversion of slaves. Unconverted they presented no problem, since the slave owner would not be holding a fellow Christian as a slave. But theologians and clergymen said it was the Christian's obligation to teach slaves Christianity and convert them . Some Southerners resolved the issues by defining the blacks as less than human. We don't convert dogs, Kudus, or zebras; therefore, we don't need to convert blacks as a lower animal form, they lack soul to be saved. And so the controversy went on. Ultimately, a compromise was reached. Religious leaders abandoned their original position and said that the Church would no longer maintain the position that conversion required emancipation. This meant that the Church could save souls and the slave owners their investments. This compromise led to substantial missionary activity among the slaves, who were rapidly converted to Christianity, since of course, they had little choice on the matter.[87]

It is indeed unfortunate that the Christian Church had to get itself entangled in an enterprise so devilish and inhuman. Such reflects the nature of the hypocritical Christianity that some segments of people aimed to be genuine. Concerning this, Chapman Cohen says:

> In nearly every case the enslavers professed Christian religion, they conquered Black people and justified their evil actions on the ground that they were the owner of pure religion and higher civilization. In my researches, such damnable segregation on the basis of color has not been practiced among the people of antiquity. Neither the people of Ancient Near East, nor Africans

themselves knew it. As proud as the Greeks such color line never existed. The Greeks highly respect the Africans as men of wisdom and the most courageous, tallest and handsome people on earth. Without question, this color ban essentially belongs to the Christian time.

The peculiar and damning fact in the history of slavery (as pointed out by a careful student of the institution), so far as the Christian Church is concerned, ... (is that) it was created by Christians, it was continued by Christians, it was in some respects more barbarous than anything the world had yet seen, and its worst features were to he witnessed in countries that were most ostentatious in their parade of Christianity. It is this that provides the final and unanswerable indictment of the Christian Church . . . . It should be added that, according to Livingstone, slavery was unknown to the Africans until it was introduced by Christians - the Portuguese.[88]

In discussing this African slave trade, an outstanding Christian and apologist, the Reverend Loring Brace, is correct when he says "The guilt of this great crime rests on the Christian Church as an organized body."[89] This is true because the Christian Church has not totally purged itself of this notion of Black inferiority - in the name of God and the Bible. The damages that this institution of slavery, begun by Christians and continued by Christians seem irreparable to African and African Americans and African children all over the globe. It is hopeful that, one day, God will open people's eyes to see the truth of how damnable the maintenance of color line is.

Summary

In a brief summary, what we have discussed so far concerning the historical heritage of the African Americans is that Africa American people definitely have a glorious heritage. Human life began among their ancestors; they are the originator of civilization, the art of writings, religion, iron smelting, and science. The Africa American ancestors built powerful Empires; they ruled the world and established university life. However, the intruders, namely Europeans, Americans, and Arabs (in service of Europeans came, kidnapped the people, stole their resources, and destroyed their civilization. The importance of knowing this

Historical Heritage

information is the fact that we should know that we Africans and African Americans are not what we were told we are. We were once successful, and it is evident that we can still be successful. All we need is discipline love, respect and hard work, for God has given us all the potential we need.

Endnotes

[1] David B. Guralnik, ed. "Black," *Webster's New World Dictionary*, 2nd ed. (New York, Simon and Schulster, 1980), 146.

[2] Ibid., 1621. I am grateful to Pauline Logan who called my attention to Webster's definition of Black and White.

[3] R.L Johnstone, *Religion and Society in Interaction* (Englewood Cliffs: Prentice-Hall, Inc., 1975), 218.

[4] (Boston: Beacon Press, 1958), 1-2.

[5] No 6 and 7 are from my observation.

[6] "The Negro Family in the United States," (Book Review), *American journal of Sociology*, 14: 799, 1940. *The Negro Church in America* (New York: Shocken Books, 1966) 1-2.

[7] Arthur Weigall, *Personlities of Antiquity* (Garden City: NY: Doubleday, Doran & Co., Inc., 1928), 185-192.

[8] *Introduction to Black Studies* (Los Angeles, California: Kawaida Publications, 1983), 47-52.

[9] Ibid. 49.

[10] Ibid. 50.

[11] Ibid.50.

[12] Ibid. 51.

[13] Cited by Ivor Wilks, "African Historiographic Traditions, Old and New," in *Africa Discover Her Past*, edited by J.D Fage (London: Oxford University Press, 1970), 7.

[14] Ibid. 1

[15] Cited by Ashley Montagu, *Man's Most Dangerous Myth* (New York: Oxford University Press, 1974), 7.

[16] *A Study of History*, vol. 1 (Oxford University Press, 1968), 235.

[17] R. L Johnstone, *Religion and Society in Interaction*, 218.

[18] Charles Darwin, *Descent of Man* (New York: Modern Library Edition, Random House, 1871), 520.

[19] Albert Churchward, *The Origin and Eeevolution of the Human Race*, cited by John G. Jackson, *Introduction to African Civilization* (Secaucus, New Jersey: The Citadel Press, 1970), 41.

[20] E. A Wallis Budge, *The Egyptian Sudan, Its History and Monuments*, vol.1 (New York:

AMS Press, 1976 Reprint) 512-513.

[21] Diodorus, 3:11, 3:2-3:7.

[22] Quoted by Ronoko Rashidi, "African Presence in Ancient Summer and Elam," *Egypt Revisited*, edited by I V. Sertima (New Brunswick: Journal of African Civilization, 1982),140.

[23] C.F Volney, *The Ruins of Empires* (New York: Peter Eckler, 1890), 17.

[24] Sir E. A Wallis Budge, *The Egyptian Sudan*, vol 1, 512-513, and vol. 2, 415-416; Sir Henry Rawlinson,, cited by John G. Jackson, *Ethiopia and the Origin of Civilization* (Baltimore: Black Classic Press, 1939), 11-13. Richard Lepsius, cited by Ronoko Rashidi, in *Egypt Revisited*, edited by I. V Sertima, Journal of African Civilization, Inc. 1982, 140.

[25] Fllinders Petrie, *The Making of Egypt* (London: Seldon Press, 1939), 68-69.

[26] Cited by J.G. Jackson, *Man, God and Civilization*, 194. C.E. Volney, The Ruins of Empires, ; E. A Hooten Up *from the Ape* (new York: The Macmillan Co., 1931) 591-592.

[27] Hooten, *Up From the Ape*, 591-592.

[28] Ibid. , 179.

[29] Arthur Weigall, *Personalities of Antiquity*, 185-192. Some scholars who think that nothing good can come from Africa, denounced Piankhi's claim as a propoganda.

[30] Ibid.

[31] Ibid.

[32] Ibid.

[33] Ivan Van Sertima, They Came Before Columbus (New York: Random House, 1976), 14. I will like to acknowledge my indebtedness to Sertima for this information in this section.

[34] Ibid.

[35] *They Came*, 56.

[36] James Pritchard, ed. *Ancient Near Eastern Text relating to the Old Testament* (ANET) (Princeton: Princeton University Press, 1969), 265-268. Although soe scholars freuse all the overwhelming evidence which identify Magan and Meluhha with Egypt and Ethiopia, I think that it i rasonably certain that Magan and Meluhha should be located in Africa.

[37] J.B Thatcher, Christopher Columbus: His Life, His Work, His Remains (New York: G.P Putnam's Sons, 1903), vol. 1 , 665.

[38] According to Sertima, the word gua-nin is a West African word which means gold and it was passed to the Indians through trade contact. See *They Came*, 11-12

[39] Ibid.

[40] Ibid., 14 .

[41] Ibid.

[42] Arthur J. Weise, *Discoveries of America to 1525* (New York: G. P Putman's Sons, 1884), 225-228.

[43] Cited by Sertima, *They Came*, 21.

[44] F.A MacNutt (ed) and translated), DE Orbo Novo: The Eight Decades of Peter Martyr d'Anghera (New York:1912), Sertima quoted from the above book 21-22.

[45] Sertima, *They Came*, 33

[46] Ibid.265,

[47] *Herodotus*, Translated by Sir Henry Rawlinson, Book III, 20, and III :114.

[48] Peter DeRoo, *History of America Before Columbus*, 2 vol.s. (Philadelphia: J.B Lippincott, 1900), 306-307. See also Jackson 233-234, Sertima, *They Came*, 23 See also Alphonse de Quatrefages, The Huan Species (New York: Appleton & Co., 1905) 200.

[49] Alexandre Braghine, *The Shadow of Atlantis* (New York: E.P Dutton & Co., 1940), 40-41.

[50] Ibid.

[51] Robert Wanchope, " A Tentative Sequence of the Pre Classic Ceramics in Middle America," **Tulane University, Middle American Research Institute,**, Publication 15,

1950, 238.
[52] Sertima, *They Came*, 144-145.
[53] M. W Sterling, "Discovering the New World's Oldest Dated Work of Man," in *National Georgraphic Magazine*, vol. 76 (Aug. 1939), 183-218.
[54] Sertima, *They Came,* 148.
[55] Ibid.
[56] Ibid., 157-158 and 161.
[57] Jackson, *Introduction to African Civilization,* 253.
[58] A.H Verill, *Old Civilizations of the New World* (New York: Tudor

Publishing Co., 1938),143-146.

[59] Sertima, *They Came*, 265.
[60] J. A Rogers, *Sex and Race*, vol I (New York: Rogers Publishers, 1942), 270.
[61] Sertima, *They Came,* 265.
[62] Ibid.
[63] Ibid.
[64] Jackson, *Introduction*, 300-301.
[65] Ibid.
[66] Ibid.
[67] Jackson, *Introduction*, 19.
[68] Sir Henry H Johnston, *A History of the Colonization of Africa*, 78-79.
[69] Jackson, *Introduction*, 305.
[70] Ibid.
[71] Basil Davidson, *The African Past*, 136.
[72] J.C DeGAft-Johnson, *African Glory: of Vanished Negro Civilization* (New York: Walker & Co. 1966), 152.

[73] Stanton A Colentz, *The Long Road to Humanity* (New York: Thomas Yoseloff, 1959), 325.
[74] DeGraft-Johnson, *African Glory*, 157.
[75] Jackson, *Introduction,* 311.
[76] Ibid.,154.
[77] E.B. D'Auvergne, *Human Livestock*, 68-69.

[79] DeGraft-Johnson, *African Glory*, 155.
[80] Ibid.
[81] Ibid.
[82] Ibid., 155-156.
[83] Jackson, *Introduction*, 304-305.
[84] Chapman Cohen, *Christianity, Slavery and Labour* (London: The Pioneer Press, 1936), 55.
[85] *Report of the Anti-Slavery Society in Interaction* (New York: 1860), 281.
[86] Jackson, *Introduction*, 309.
[87] R. L Johnstone, *Religion, and Society in Interaction*, 218.
[88] Jackson, *Introduction*,305.
[89] Joshep McCabe, *The Social Record of Christianity* (London: Watts and Co. 1935), 94.

Chapter III

AFRICAN-AMERICAN RELIGIOUS HERITAGE

In the preceding chapter, I discussed the historical heritage of the African American people. In this chapter, I do not intend to enumerate and explain the various African divinities and religious practices that have been brought over and practiced by the African Diaspora in America during the pre-Columbian presence and slavery. My main concern here is to discuss some essential characteristics and nature of African Traditional Religion before and after the coming of the foreign domination. The similar characteristics that are visible in the African-American religious experience in the United States will be discussed. My readers need to understand that the people whom we have in mind are typical, ordinary Africans and African American people rather than the few sophisticated ones in the cities who have almost totally embraced the Western life-style at the expense of their heritage. The following are some of these characteristics of religion among the Africans and African Americans: Communality, Action Oriented ness, Inseparability of Religious and the secular, and Priesthood.

Inseparability of Religious from the Secular

The richest and the most important heritage of Africa is religion. This heritage permeates the entire life of the African people. This heritage has dominated the thinking of African people to the extent that it shapes their cultural, social, political and economic activities. It has also shaped all aspects of African life to the extent that it becomes so difficult to separate what is religious from what can be considered secular.

In African life, especially before the coming of the White domination of Africa, the Divine is consulted in almost every occasion. This is very true among the Yoruba people of Nigeria. Immediately when there is a conception, religion is involved. The pregnant woman quickly consults the native priest who in turn consults the divine oracles to know either what sex the child would be or what type of life the child will live. Sometimes what type of name the child would have would reflect its life. When a child is born, the parent not only would consult the priest and the divine oracle to know what names are to be given, they also find out how successful the child will be in life. In many occasions, the child is given a theophoric name (a divine name after the gods) to express appreciation to the god, who is believed to have helped in providing the child. Examples of these names are Ogungberni (god supports me), Osayomi (Osa delivers me. This is my mother's name), Ogunbode (god has come), Oluyomi (God delivers me), and others. More will be said on names in the next chapter.

At the time of initiation into adulthood, religious ceremonies and sacrifices are performed with prayers and consultation with the divinities. When a wife is to be chosen, the priest and the divinities are also consulted; sacrifices are also offered to make sure that the right wife is chosen. Other major events in which the consultation of the gods is crucial is choosing a chief and during sickness. Before a leader or a king is chosen, in order to be sure that he will live long and be a good king, the priest, who in turn consults the divinities, is consulted. I witnessed such occasions in my village in Isanlu, Kogi State, Nigeria. When the Agbana of Isanlu died, two people were qualified to be Agbana (Ikuborije and Ekunode, respectively). Ikuborije has a Grade II teacher's certificate, while Ekunode has a lesser education. Only one of them would be the Agbana of Isanlu. Although the community believed that Ikuborije is more educated or enlightened, the argument against him is that the Ifa Oracle says that he will not live long enough, but that Ekuriode will and that he will bring prosperity to the town. However, Ikuborije became the Agbana of Isanlu. In the time of sickness, the first thing to do is to consult the priest, who consults the divinity for the cause of the sickness. The reason is that there is always a suspicion of whether the sick person has Offended one of the gods. If there is evidence of offense, it is believed that no matter what medicine is applied to the sickness, the person will never be cured.

Other areas of life in which such consultation and involvement with the African divinities are crucial are the time of traveling, the time of choosing land for farming, the time of learning a trade, and the time of other important things. The most important divinity that is frequently consulted among the Yoruba people is Ifa Oracle.

The Beginning of African-American Church

From the above cultural environments the African American people came to the Americas as early as 800 B. C. (if we accept the Carbon 14 dating of

Religious Heritage

the stone head mentioned previously). The worship of African gods and the practices of African ceremonial rites to which they were exposed at home continued to influence their way of life not only in South America but also in the United States.

During he early days of slavery in the United States the first batch of slaves who arrive in America in 1619 were not void of religion. They also brought with them their African religious heritage. Such religious heritage involved a faith with strong belief in One Supreme Being who is above all things, and who ha delegated his powers to other divinities to take care of the affairs of the world. They practiced this religion in secret because of the fair of their masters.

The African American church did not come into being until the end of the late seventeenth century, when the slaves masters reluctantly introduced Christianity to the African slaves in America with the erroneous thought that it would make them better slaves. To achieve such objective, the most popular Bible texts were taken from the book of Philemon. The Book of Philemon in the New Testament Christian Bible was one of Paul's letters to a slave master called Philemon. Paul pleaded with Philemon on behalf of Onesimus, the slave. There Paul emphasized to Philemon, Onesimus' master, that Onesimus had changed and that he would be a good slave. When these African were not allowed to worship with the White masters, they resorted to worshipping secretly and their worship was mixed with elements of Christianity and African Traditional Religion. Despite the persecution, the service went on. Although there were slaves in America during the eighteenth century, the largest influx of African slaves to Christianity took place in the first half of the nineteenth century.

In the early development of the African-American church, many White Churches excluded the slaves. Those who did not exclude them required that they sit in the balcony and receive the Lord's Supper in the basement. This practice still continued even after the American Civil War. Yet, as early as 1700 there were African-American preachers who preached to predominantly white congregations.[1] Among these preachers are Lemuel Haynes of Connecticut, and Richard Allen of Philadelphia. They regarded him as the most famous of the African-American preachers. Richard Allen preached at St. George Methodist Episcopal Church (a predominantly white Church). The numbers of the African-American people grew substantially in St. George Methodist Episcopal Church. African Americans were removed from the seats around the walls and ordered to sit in the gallery.

Religious Heritage

"Mistaking the section of the gallery which they were to occupy," Richard Allen, Absalom Jones, and another member were almost dragged from their knees when praying.[2] They left the church and established the 'Free African Society. " From the 'Tree African Society" came the establishment of the African Methodist Episcopal Church and African Protestant Episcopal Church of St. Thomas by Allen and Jones respectively. However, in the South, the African-Americans continued to join their master's churches in great numbers, namely Methodists, Baptists, and Presbyterians. They continued to worship in the segregated sections of their masters' churches. When the question of slave status reached its peak, the Presbyterians, the Episcopalians, Baptists and Methodists built separate Churches for Black slaves. The example of the establishment of these Churches was followed throughout the nation.

From the above, it is evident that the establishment of these African American churches carne in response to slavery, racism and segregation. The African-Americans who found it difficult to reconcile the message of the white church with the institution of slavery, racism and segregation had no choice but to establish their own Church. The search for identity, leadership, and personhood also led to the establishment of these African American churches. This great search for identity involves mostly the freedom to worship in their own ways a way, which reflects their religious heritage from Africa. This African religious heritage is the religious involvement in all facets of life without which is called today "the separation of the Church and the State."

When this freedom was finally won, the church became everything to the African American community. The Church became an agency of social control, a means of economic cooperation, a school for educating the public, an arena of political life, and, finally, a refuge in a hostile world.[3]

The church as an agency of social control bears the burden of morality. Loose life, which had been created by the separation among African American slaves of husbands and wives, the prohibition of marriage among slaves, and emancipation after the Civil War. The Church, through power exercised by the minister, became a means by which this uncontrolled life was regulated.

The churches also began to pool their meager resources together, so that the African-American community could be employed and cared for in times of sickness and death. After the Civil War in 1897, societal organizations to cater for these people were also formed.

To the Church, the African American community owes its early means

Religious Heritage

of education. The churches pooled together their resources and established schools. Some churches actually became schools where the African-American people learned how to read and write at the elementary, secondary and even university levels.

The most obvious area in which the lack of separation between the religious and the secular is certainly visible is in the area of political life among African American people. As in Africa, the native priests and the oracles had to be consulted before any king could be installed, or any important decision is made, politics have been a part and parcel of the African-American Church in America.

When African Americans were excluded from white dominated political activities, the church became the arena of political activities. The church became the place where their aspirations for leadership could be fulfilled. The struggle for power could be satisfied in the church. The church itself has a political meaning to the African-American community. When the African Americans were denied the right to vote, one thing was certain, they could exercise the right of voting in the Church during the election of their leaders (Bishops, Pastors, and elders).

When African American people needed to fight for their political, social, and economic rights, they turned to the Church. This is partly because, as it was in Africa, the church is the center of the people's lives. Not only the "citadel of faith," the church has also been an economic entity, a "political powerbase, a cultural vehicle," and a reservoir of leadership to the African-American community. "All African American churches have a common characteristic -they are more than a church' and they are multifaceted cultural, social, and religious entities. They represent a home away from home for African American people. The churches act as centers of information and are reservoirs of power for African American people seeking identity and purpose.[4]

It is undeniable that the African American Church provided most of the leadership needed for the Civil Rights movement. The African American church was one of the real earliest organizations, which protested against slavery in America. This same church provided the leadership needed to combat the evil institution.

African American Churches gave birth to most of the predominantly African-American organizations established for the Civil Rights movement. The oldest and the most active of these African American Civil Rights organizations is the National Association for the Advancement of Colored

Religious Heritage

People (NAACP). NAACP and the Urban League are greatly indebted to African-American Church. It is not an exaggeration to say that their achievements and even their existence would have been impossible without the Church. Even now, one of every three officers of the NAACI? is a preacher. Many regard the NAACP as the fighting arm of the church. It is no surprise that African American in their struggle during the 1950's and 1960's chose an African-American preacher from Alabama (Martin Luther King, Jr.) to be their chief spokesman and leader. He, in turn, chose African-American church, the most powerful institution among the African-American community.

Martin Luther King, Jr. formed the Southern Christian Leadership Conference (S.C.L.C.), which served as the base for his Civil Rights activities. Most of the members of the S.C.L.C. were ministers who believed in the non-violent approach to achieve justice. Later, the Student Non-Violent Coordinating Committee (SNCC) was formed in Martin Luther King, Jr.'s spirit of non-violence. The members registered voters in several African-American churches as a means of achieving their civil rights objectives. As a result of these peaceful protests and demonstrations, channeled through the church, the Civil Rights Acts of 1957 and 1964 were finally achieved.

The presidential candidacy of the Rev. Jesse Jackson in 1984 is a living testimony to the African-American church's most important role and to the fact that the religious is not divorced from the secular. The Rev. Jones' comments on Jesse Jackson's political activities are instructive about this:

> Jesse's is more than normal political effort; His is a crusade, a movement, and a revolutionary thrust that combines all that distinguishes Black life. It's a basic spirituality that reaches back to Africa; a basic sense of cohesiveness that combines with a willingness to forget caste and class.[5]

Dr. Wyatt Tee Walker believes that the Black church was behind all these movements, which finally provided for the African American people their needed freedom. He asks the following questions and provides the answer:

> What was the genesis of this movement? Who were its
> leaders? Where did the troops come from? What was the
> origin of its methodology? Where did they meet? How

Religious Heritage

> was it financed? What provided the organizational
> thrust? . . . in one way or another is the black Church.[6]

Supporting Dr. Walker, Rev. Otis Moss also believes that the Church is responsible f or the well-being and the political activities of the African-American people. He says:

> It is no accident that the Black Church has produced Much of the political leadership in the United States. And without the Black Church there would be no Black politicians. The Black Church is more important than any party could ever be.[7]

Another example of the lack of separation between the religious and the secular life of the African-American people can be given from the local community in Waco, Texas. The Reverend Cleo LaRue, a good friend of mine, and pastor of Toliver Chapel Missionary Baptist Church, Waco, Texas, has defended very gallantly, not only his Church members, but the entire African-American community in Waco. When the problem of consolidation of Waco Independent School District came up in 1983 and the schools in the African American section of the town were to be closed down, so that the African-American children would have to be bussed to the White section of the town, the Reverend LaRue, inspiring and leading other ministers, took the case to Court. Large was both a member of the Advisory Committee of the United Way and the Tri-Ethnic Committee of Waco.

Another local example is the election of Dr. Ray Shackelford to the Waco City Council in 1985. When Dr. Shackelford needed some votes, he knew where to go. He went to the African American Churches. It was the Reverend LaRue who appeared to be the most active Church leader pleading for votes in the Church. The result was not less than a victory over the opponent. It is my opinion that without the Church, he would never have won the election. The African American Church has been and is still everything to the African-American people because of its holistic ministry. More will be discussed on this under Priesthood.

All I have been saying here is that Religion permeates all life in Africa, and that concept was brilliantly transferred and transformed in to African-American Christianity. Professor C. Erie Lincoln expressed what I

Religious Heritage

life in Africa is a way of fulfilling the mission of the individual, that is, "spreading happiness," making life easier and more enjoyable.[11]

The African-American people coming from this background where life is viewed holistically, cannot but approach life that way. During the early years of slavery, the slave masters recognized this aspect of Africanness perfectly well. That was why every effort was made to separate children from their parents, brothers from brothers, wives from husbands, and those who spoke the same language from one another. Yet, there is little success in dismantling this African heritage (communality). Instead, persecution, suffering, racism, segregation and torture strengthened this heritage more than ever. This sense of oneness was guarded jealously, not only in the days of slavery but also after the Emancipation. This African American way of approaching life holistically is carried to the religion of the slave masters, which they accepted. The result was a powerful, moving, effective, and unique African American Christianity that the Whites up until today have found difficult to understand. African American Christianity was so enriched by its Africanness that the African-American Church became everything to the society. At first, slaves were forbidden to gather or express this communal heritage, but eventually the Church became a place to express it. This expression of communality resulted in very powerful movements and organizations, both religious and secular that have helped the African-American people to gain their freedom and sense of human identity. This is especially illustrated by the activities of religious leaders in the days of Martin Luther King, Jr.

It is my opinion that Africans and African-American people should keep and perpetuate their valuable heritage, which is still needed f or survival and for the welfare of our next generation.

Action-Oriented Nature of Religion

African-American Ancestors

Among the African-American ancestors, religion is not a thing to celebrate passively. Religion, as mentioned earlier, embraced the reality of life; it cannot be divorced from the secular life; it is a communal business, and it has to be expressed loudly and clearly. It has to be active. It is the characteristic of African Traditional Religion to be deeply emotional and enthusiastic. In virtually all occasions, the means to arouse the emotion is

Religious Heritage

music. No one is more affected by music than the Africans. The emotion of music is felt to the depth of their souls. The automatic response to music, especially to drums, is singing, dancing, stamping of feet, clapping of hands, and shouting. Music and religion are inseparable and they automatically stir up Africans and African Diaspora into action.

This action-oriented nature of the Africans was carried to Christianity. Music became a means of celebrating their religion brought by the missionaries. At the sound of the drum and flute in the Church, Africans had to move, stamp their feet, clap their hands, and dance. Unfortunately, the majority of the early missionaries, who thought that whatever was African was inferior, paganistic and without relevance to Christianity, forbade African music, songs and dance, because they said they were evil and idolatrous. If you have an opportunity to go to the fatherland (Africa), do not be surprised if you see an African at the sound of music throw off his jacket, jump up and shout, inside or outside the Church. This reminds me of my childhood days in my village (Irunda, East Yagba Local Government, Kogi State, Nigeria). During the evening service, the drum sounded, the people began to clap their hands, tap their feet and shout, Ogo! Ogo! fun Olugbala (Praise the Savior) . Suddenly, one of the prominent elders of the only local Baptist Church in Irunda jumped up seized the shaker and began to dance. Another elder could not resist the frenzied beat of the drum. He jumped up likewise, threw off his jacket and began to dance. Other elders followed until the entire congregation got up and began to dance for the Lord. When the pastor arrived, he stopped the congregation and asked, "What are you all doing? What if Rev. Mcgee (the White missionary, who established the Church) sees you like this? Don't you know we are Baptists? We don't dance; we don't shout."

When the SIM (Sudan Interior Mission) missionaries arrived in Nigeria, they banned their Evangelical Churches of West Africa (ECWA), from beating drums, dancing, and of clapping hands. As late as 1978, the late Osagbemi, the then Chairman of the United District Church Council of ECWA, forbade dancing and clapping of hands during the worship service at Egbe. I think it is time that the missionaries learn to understand who Africans and the African American people are. It is time that we also understand who we are d what we are ourselves. It is time that we express our Christianity the African way, as long as it does not contradict the Bible. What I am saying is that the African-American ancestors are emotional, ritualistic, fundamentally religious, and action-oriented people. When they were not allowed to express themselves the way they felt and the way they understood God, most of the mainline missionary Churches became dull, and they do not meet the deep emotional needs of the African people.

I think the establishment of the African Independent Churches is a response and a challenge to the type of worship going on in most of the mainline Churches. These African Independent Churches have freedom to express the spiritual feeling with action and deep emotion. In other words, even though they became Christians, yet remained Africans, they expressed their Christianity the African way. Canon Dr. Omoyajowo observed one of these African Independent Churches and commented on what he saw:

> It is a common place that the tremendous success of the Independent Aladura Churches in making converts is largely attributable to their use in divine services of drums, singing, clapping, dancing and stamping. . . .
> The C & S (Cherubim and Seraphim) explanation for their use of these phenomena is that they are the ode of happiness by which that order was founded, and when hey are used in divine services the members are believed to be endowed with different kinds of blessings appertaining to each action which are revealed by divine instruction as follows: clapping for victory, protection, love and providence kicking (that is stamping of the ground) for spiritual power, peace and prosperity; singing and dancing for joy, and happiness. All of these benefits are received when actions are performed simultaneously these religious expressions are reminiscent of the traditional African way of Worship.[12]

African Americans

The African American people came out of this type of environment where action and emotion are part of the totality of life. Since their ancestors possess this fundamental religious characteristic, there should be no wonder why the African American Churches are different from most of the White Churches. What the African American people brought from Africa was transferred and brilliantly fashioned to their worship services in America. This Africanism was woven into their beliefs and worship. That is why in African American Churches religious beliefs and worship are carried into action. When the music sounds, the African American people, whose feelings are easily affected by music, could not help but burst into

Religious Heritage

shouting, dancing, and emotional frenzy. It is important that my readers observe that the action-oriented nature of worship in the African American Churches is probably one of the most obvious continuity between the African and the African-American religions. This also characterizes the unique fundamental difference between the White Churches and the African American Churches; Rabteau's observation is very instructive:

> Perhaps the most obvious continuity between African and African American religions is the style of performance in ritual action. Drumming, singing, and dancing are essential features of African and Afro-American liturgical expression and are crucial to the ceremonial possession of cult members by their gods.[13]

I believe that the criticism leveled against the African American Churches that they are just "mere emotional" Churches, who do nothing but make "noise" can be understood sympathetically because this criticism is a result of ignorance rooted in prejudice. First of all, when the slave masters first went to Africa, they did not go there to understand the African American ancestors. They went there to rape the African American ancestors' homes by kidnapping, stealing, and enslaving them. Even after the Africans arrived here in chains and had the opportunity to worship with the slave masters in the same Church, African-American action-oriented nature of worship was more effective and attracted more members. The slave masters became jealous and established separate Churches for the African Americans. Those who refused to leave were forced to leave through persecution and maltreatment.

As said earlier, some of the so-called missionaries who went to Africa went there only to give and not to receive. This is because they think that nothing can be learned from the Africans, since they are savages," "barbarians" and less than human. How then does one expect such people to sit down patiently and learn how and why the African-American worship services are different from theirs? All that I am saying precisely is that the African-American method of worship has reason to be the way it is. It reveals who and what they have been and what they are. In other words, it reveals their identity and their heritage. Unless the White people sit down and study the nature of Africans and African Americans patiently, they will continue to bear false witness against their neighbors, thus breaking the Commandment (Exodus 20:16).

Religious Heritage

Priesthood

I have discussed the characteristic nature of Africans and African American religions. Such characteristics discussed are mainly: inseparability of the secular from the religious, communality, and action-oriented nature. It is important to know that these characteristics affect the nature and the function of African and African-American religious specialist that we are about to discuss below.

African-American Ancestors' Priesthood

In all religions of the world, one finds sacred specialists who are in charge of certain important rituals. The fact that the sacred is dangerous, mysterious and contagious requires that a specialist who is an expert handle it. The sacred specialist in African Traditional Religious belief has been variously called: sorcerer, juju-man, witch doctor and others. These African sacred specialists are wrongly called the above names because of the ignorance rooted in prejudice and racism that have plagued some outside observers, writers, and scholars.

These sacred specialists are priests of African Religion. These priests are to be found in places where the gods are worshipped. As in the Old Testament, the office of priesthood may be hereditary. In this case, a priest is set aside for his service from birth. He is then constantly involved with this service as he grows up. Parents may also offer their children for the service of gods in which case the children become priests for life. A priest may also be suddenly called to service through spirit-possession. When such a person is called, he withdraws from his occupation and undergoes rigorous training under an older priest. Such training may last several years until he masters the secret of consulting and serving the gods. This training involves a strict observance of special chastity, taboos and actions that may make him closer to the spirit. The gaining of special knowledge of "medical medicines," counseling, prayer, and the act of prophecy is important. Women may also be priestesses in African Traditional Religion, like that of the Old Testament (Huldah and Anna, II Kings 22:14; 11 Chron. 34:22). They may work in conjunction with male priests or independently.

Among the Yoruba people of Nigeria, the priests are called *Aworo* or *Babalawo* . They are in charge of worship of the divinities. Dr. Awolalu emphasizes the fact that "Each divinity in Yorubaland has his or her own priesthood."[14] For example, the priest of Orisa-nla presides at the worship of Orisa-nla; Sango priest at the worship of Sango; Alayelala's priest at the worship of Alayelala.

Generally, priests, especially among the Yoruba people of Nigeria, are in a class among themselves in the villages and cities. The priest who holds the highest rank may be called Olori-Awo or Oba Awo.[15] This may be like the high priest in the Old Testament. In most villages and cities this class exists. Whenever there is a problem (disease or evil) that could not be solved by the lesser priest, it is the duty of the lesser priests to refer the problem to the Olori-Awo or Oba-Awo. Any newly arrived priest to a city or village, must first of all give special regard to the Olori-Awo of the city or village before beginning his priestly work. As mentioned earlier, there is no separation between the Church and the State or the religious and the secular in African society. The priests are involved with every department of the life of African society. The priests conduct the business of worship when the devotees gather for worship, declare god's will and pleasure, and offer sacrifices. They are also involved in political areas of life. Before any chief or king or any leader of the people is chosen, the priests are consulted. These leaders draw their power of authority from the priests. The priests are involved in the political, cultural, religious, social, and economic life of the people. They are visible representatives of gods. They are also prophets, traditional healers, comforters, and deliverers of the community from the evil forces which plague them during village disasters, sickness, war, pestilence, childbirth, bereavement, and political upheaval. This almost unlimited role of the priests among the African people has made them indispensible to the community. They command deep respect and reverence. To them is ascribed automatic competence, because they are representative of the divinity. Their presence is a relief to the bereaved. They have access to almost every place in African society.

African American Priesthood

During the early days of slavery, those who became leaders of the slaves were people who had close knowledge of African priesthood. There were also those who claimed to have special ability, not only to lead, but also to have special contact with the divine and to be able to perform African religious ceremonies. Most of these leaders were children or relatives of the African priests. Like that of the African priests, these leaders have unlimited power over their fellow. The slave masters could only hinder this unlimited role.

When the African slaves were converted to Christianity, such unlimited roles of the priests were carried over to their type of Christianity. Like the African priests, the African American ministers involved very deeply in every aspect of life's situations of their community, not only in the religious life, but the political, social and religious life of their community. Such a role of the African American ministers is also due to the fact that African religion knows nothing of a rigid demarcation between the natural and the supernatural.[16] The fact that the Church has been the center of African American community has been discussed earlier. These facts have led the ministers during the days of slavery to place significant and crucial role on the political, economic, social and cultural development of the African American community as a whole.

The African American pastor is not only the leader of the Church, but of the African American community as a whole. He plays a symbolic role. Like the African priest, he is the "articulator of theological world view;" he is the presider over the rituals and monies, which sustain the African American community. He expounds the faith of the community in such a way that it will help the persons facing hardship to cope with it. The presence of the African American minister automatically carries an implicit message. It reminds the people not only that they are God's children, but also that the minister is the representative of God, and therefore symbolizes God's absence or hiddenness."[17] His presence then automatically evokes strong, positive and negative responses. His presence gives "a continuing affirmation of the community's identity, its goals, its values and purpose."[18]

The African-American pastor, as a leader of the Church, is also expected to provide some leadership authority to the entire community. Because of this, he is assigned wisdom and competence in every aspect of life. He is expected to display no kind of weakness, and to he omniscient, omnipotent and omnipresent in solving every earthly problem of his people[19]

Although no one can live up to those expectations, the African American pastor has no choice but to strive to live up to them by virtue of the importance of his or her office in the community. The community also draws its power of authority from the African American Church, led by the minister. Because of this symbolic role of the African American pastor, he is accorded the greatest respect among the community. When comparing such a role with the white pastor among his people, the uniqueness of the

Religious Heritage

African American pastor comes out very clearly and this is due to the African religious heritage. Although diminishing these days, it is remarkable that this role, which had been ingrained in the blood of their ancestors, the African-Americans are able to adapt to the American situation. The Rev. Jones observes this uniqueness of the African American minister, which can he traced back to Africa. Although this has been quoted earlier, it is important to quote it again:

According to him Jesse's political effort is "a crusade, a movement, a revolutionary thrust that combines all that distinguished black life." It is a spirituality that has its root from Africa. His candidacy is a demonstration of a clear radical difference "between the Black church and the white church, between the Black preacher and the White preacher." The Black preacher has a kind of freedom that the White preacher has never known.

That nobody has been given such a free role and so much respect in America is emphasized by Edward P. Wimberly »[20] W. E. B. DuBoise was also emphatic on the unique role and authority given to the African-American minister. He said:

The preacher is the most unique personality developed by the Negro on American soil. A leader, a politician, an orator, a boss,' an intriguer, and idealist - all these he is, and ever, too, the center of a group of men, now twenty, now a thousand in number. The combination of a certain adroitness with deep-seated earnestness, of tact with consummate ability, gave him his preeminence, and helps him to maintain it.[21]

The style of preaching of the American-American minister is another area in which their African religious heritage is evident. The African American pulpit is symbolic. It is a symbol of freedom. It is a place where the oppressed people burst out of bounds that have entrapped them all week. The pastor, as the most visible symbol of that freedom, burst out and used every possible means when preaching to express such unlimited freedom. The Black pastor burst into shouts and sometimes into ecstasy as he preaches. His method of sermon delivery becomes rhythmical, melodic, regular and with more unrestrained pattern or behavior than the White preacher.[22]

At this stage, his sermon becomes a song to be chanted. The congregation usually shares in this experience of freedom as they are also moved into frenzy like the Africans who are possessed by the spirits of the gods. In many cases, such unrestrained behavior is discouraged, or ignored, but accepted and shared by the entire congregation. Such is regarded as an

Religious Heritage

expression of people's feeling of frustration, which individuals have experienced. In African American worship, this emotional outward expression is therapeutic. The acceptance and sharing of such feeling, by holding sympathetically, makes the individuals feel that they are loved and cared for. This style of sermon delivery and the people's response to it is rooted in the fact that African people are action-oriented people. They view life holistically. This is also rooted in the nature of African traditional religious worship, which involves action and songs, drums and dance. The art of story-telling in sermon delivery is also rooted in the fact that African people, especially the priests, are good story-tellers. Before the priests are initiated, they have to learn, not only some specific action or ritual action, but they also learn special songs, dances, short poetry and stories. The whole African culture is full of all the above. It is therefore a very remarkable thing that the African Americans have been able to adapt their traditional African religion to their Christianity and to the ghetto situation to form a very powerful, relevant and unique Christianity. It will not be an exaggeration, therefore, to say that what makes the African-American preaching styles and Christianity so unique from their White counterpart is the adaptation of this African culture and religion into their Christianity and experience. Such should be kept and should continue to be used effectively.

Summary

In order to understand the religion and attitude of the African American people, there is a need to understand their African religious heritage. This is because their heritage from Africa, brilliantly transformed, recreated and applied to Christianity makes the religion of the African Americans unique. This African religious heritage includes the lack of demarcation between religion and the secular, the communal and the action oriented nature of religion, and the concept of priesthood. In other words, religion affects the totality of life. The African American minister should therefore continue to use this heritage effectively in every situation that applies to the African American community. This is very appropriate because:

> . . . any religion that professes to be concerned with the souls of men and ignores the social and economic conditions that cripple the soul is a spiritually morbid and dead religion only waiting to be buried. It is the duty of all ministers to make the gospel

Religious Heritage

relevant, and in almost every community, it is the Negro minister who is at the forefront of protests.[23]

African American Ancestors' Religion

Having discussed the characteristics of the African American ancestors' religion, it is appropriate to discuss what exactly that religion is all about. This is important because it affects the entire life of Africans and African Americans, especially in their religious life.

The Yoruba people have a complex religious system and a complex concept of the universe. These can be illustrated in the form of "pyramidal structure as shown below.

GOD (*Olodumare*)

DIVINITIES (*Orisas*)

SPIRITS (*Emi*)

ANCESTORS (The Living Dead)

KINGS, PRIESTS, CHIEFS, QUEENS, RULERS, Devotee

The occupant of the highest place is God who is the Supreme Being called *Olorun* or *Olodumare*. The Divinities are called *Orisas* and occupy the second level in Yoruba religious system. The third position in the order of things belongs to the spirits called *Emi*. The ancestors who are referred to as the "Living-Dead" occupy the fourth position. They are not considered supernatural beings like he occupants of the first, second, and third positions. Special human beings who are rulers, kings, priests, queens, and chiefs are in the fifth position. They are living beings. The devotees occupy the sixth place.

In my discussion of African worldview, attention would be given to African medicine. The meaning, classification, and the use of it will be discussed. I consider this to be very important because the reading and interpretation of the Bible in African Indigenous churches have some affinities with African medicine.

God

Like the Biblical Hebrew, the existence of God in Africa is assumed. In fact, the question of the existence of God is not disputed. The idea that He is the creator of the heavens and earth and of human being is not disputed in African Indigenous religion. This idea of Him as the creator and the final authority is expressed in the names given to Him in Africa. For example, the Yoruba people of Nigeria call Him *Olodumare* which means He is Almighty and supreme; *Olorun*, the owner of heaven; *Eleda*, the creator and maker; *Alaaye*, the living One; *Elemi*, the owner of spirit or breath. Among the Yoruba people of Nigeria, it is believed that these names of God are potent. It is believed that these names could perform some miracles and bring blessing. Among the Ibos of Nigeria, He is called *Chineke*, creator; *Onyeokike*, the person who creates; *Chukwu*, Great Spirit; *Osebuluwa*, Lord who upholds the world. Among the Sierra Leonians He is called *Leve*- supreme creator, the one who is high up; *Ngewo*- God, Great Spirit. Among the Ghanians He is called *Onyame*-The Supreme Being, the creator of all things; *Mawu*-God *Mawuga*- the Great God; *Se*- The Supreme God. There are so many names of God in African indigenous tradition that we cannot name all of them here.[24]

His attributes are also many. He is the creator of the heavens and the earth. He is also in control of all things. He knows and sees all things. He is all-powerful. Even though He is far away He is also present everywhere. He is the first and the last cause. He is a spirit and can appear to human being at any time and in any place. He is king. He is judge and immortal. He is holy. Among the Yoruba people of Nigeria these attributes are expressed in songs, dances, adages, ritual actions, and others. He can use any means to heal, to protect and to deliver, to punish and to bless. He is the final protector. He can use water, sand, prayers, potent words, wood, plant, leaves, angels, man or woman to protect, to heal and to bring success. He is the king and master. His name is sacred. The names He gives to things are sacred. It is quite remarkable that there is no image of God. Unlike the Eurocentric concept of God, He is not a philosophical entity.

Religious Heritage

Belief in Divinities

According to African Traditional belief, the divinities are said to be brought into being by the Deity. The divinities are usually called Orisas in Yoruba religion. They were created to serve the Olodumare theocratic world. Sometimes the Yoruba people do not make any clear-cut distinction between the Orisas and the Spirit beings. They are considered to be both divine and live in the spirit world. They can be identified as primordial beings because some of them are said to have been with the Supreme Being long before the creation of the earth and human beings. Others are some historical figures such as kings, cultural heroes and heroines, war champions, founders of cities and others who have distinguished themselves in the community where they lived. These people have been deified. Others are mere personification of natural forces and phenomena such as earth, wind, trees, river, lagoon, sea, rock, hills and mountains. In Yoruba religion, Orisanla was regarded as partaking in the attributes of Olodumare, the Supreme Being. Some of these divinities are widely worshipped. But others are only of local importance. After God has created the entire universe, He leaves the rest of the creation in the hand of Orisanla, who becomes His Deputy-General to fashion it the way he likes. It is also believed that divinities are derivatives of the Deity. The divinities are not absolute but dependent upon Deity. This means that without the Deity, the divinities have no existence of their own.

The divinities have their own names everywhere. Most of these names are descriptions. They are also functionaries in the universe They are ministers who act as intermediaries between the Deity and man. These divinities also have categories. They may be divinities of heaven or part of the Deity's attributes. Some are either heroes or ancestral divinities. They are considered very important as far as the orderly function of the universe is concerned.

Primordial Divinities.

The divinities that are classified as primordial divinities among the Yoruba people of Nigeria are Obatala or Orisa-nla, Orunmila, Oduduwa, Esu, and Ogun.

Obatala is among the earliest divinities created by the Supreme Beings. As said above he is the arch-divinity of the Yoruba cult and as such he is widely acknowledged all over Yoruba land. His functions including giving children to barren women and molding the shape of such children in

Religious Heritage

the womb when women are pregnant. This is why this divinity is called the "sculptor divinity." The Yoruba people believe that the albinos, the dwarfs, the hunchbacks, the cripples and the dumb are created by Orisa-nla in order to make them sacred to him. He also made those who are pretty and handsome people who must thank Orisa-nla for their beauty.

Orisa-nla is noted for purity. His image is robed in pure white. All the priests and priestesses are robed in white apparel. It means that the worshippers of Obatala must be clean and upright in what they do. They may wear different color of any cloth, but the most acceptable one for Obatala is white cloths, white beads and white lead anckles and bracelets. At its worship temple, there is always a pot containing pure water fetched from the spring every morning. A virgin or a woman who has passed the age of bearing children must fetch this pure water. When carrying the water early morning, she must not greet any one before she reaches the sanctuary.

The worshippers are forbidden from making any blood sacrifices to Obatala. They must not drink anything alcoholic. No shedding of blood. Purity is the norm.

Orunmila is another primordial divinities that were asked to accompany Obatala to the earth when sent by Olodumare to be his adviser and counselor. He moves freely between the earth and heaven. That is why the Yoruba people called Orunmila *gbaye gborun* (the one who lives in both) heaven and earth. Because he moves freely between heaven and earth, he is in the position to plead with Olodumare to change any bad or unpleasant event to a good one in the life of the devotee. He is also popularly known as the oracle divinity. The way in which the oracle is ascertained is through *ifa*. He is known to be gifted with wisdom. He wonders around teaching people wisdom. By his wisdom he knows the taste and the taboo of the other divinities His priest is called the father of mysteries-*babalawo*.

Oduduwa is seen not only as a primordial being but also as an ancestor. There is no one consistent tradition about who he is exactly. One tradition says that he was the one who eventually created the earth because of the failure of Obatala who got drunk. Others says that Oduduwa was a name given to some wanderers hunters who came to the city of Ife long after the city has been created and peopled. They came and conquered the city, settled there and multiplied. Another tradition says that he is the wife of Obatala and the chief of the female divinities.

Esu is another divinity of the Yoruba people of Nigeria. He was regarded as the instructor of Orunmila. Esu in Yoruba religion is not the

Religious Heritage

total embodiment of evil as some scholars think. Esu is a special relation officer to Olodumare. He maintains good contact with Orunmila for his wisdom and good contact with Olodumare in heaven. He reports the evil plans of men and divinities to God. He tempts and punishes the offenders. He instigates human being to offend the divinities so that they can be punished. The place of his dwelling is in the household.

He must be propitiated first so that he does not make the household to be in fire. He is kept in the house to help ward off evil things and bring prosperity instead. There is no regular priesthood because of his association with other divinities. He is indeed a personification of good and evil.

Ogun is another primordial divinities, which Yoruba tradition sees as the one who makes good path for people. It was believe among the Yoruba people that when the divinities were coming to the earth, there was a thick and impassable forest which no divinity could cut through. It was Ogun with his sharp machet that came and makes a path through the thick forest for the divinities to pass to the earth. For this reason, he is highly respected by all the divinities. When difficulties come to the Yoruba people's way, appeal is made to Ogun. He clears the way or removes barriers. Some traditions associate him with Oduduwa as his ferocious son who helped him fight his enemies. It is also believed that Ogun stands for absolute justice. As a result he is called upon to witness a covenant or any binding agreement. His shrine is always outside in the open air. Other human divinities include Sango, Orisa-Oko, and Ayelala. They became divinities after their death.

Belief in Ancestors

The Yorubas, like any other Africans, believe in the active existence of the deceased ancestors. They know that death does not write finish to human life but that the earthly life has been extended into life beyond and into that place which is believed to be the abode of the departed souls.[25]

Although to say that the dead are living seems contradictory, yet it is a firm belief among most indigenous African people. The Yoruba people of Nigeria understand the fact that there is the indestructible part of humankind, which outlives the physical death. This part is the soul.

Ancestor means a father or mother from whom a person descends, at the any distance time. He or she may be one's progenitor of forefather.

However, when Africans speak of ancestors, they refer to the departed spirits of their forebear with who the living maintain constant communication and affectionate relationship. It is certain that not every person who dies become ancestor. To qualify as ancestor, one must have lived a good life, attained an old age before dying, and must have some offspring and much good memory. All who died a bad death, and children cannot become ancestors.

A person's father or mother becomes the most important figure in the spirit world. They are seen as the one who link the individual to the lineage ancestors. They link the individual with the ancestors of the past generation who live in the spirit world. The ancestors return to the living through reincarnation and to be born as a grandchild of the departed. This is done to demonstrate the love the departed has for the family presently living in the world because the world is the best place to live. Sometimes the ancestors are venerated.

It is an indisputable tact that the fear of the dead is common throughout Africa. There is also a universal belief that there can be some kind of special communion between the departed and the living. The departed can exercise certain influence on the living relatives. This writer has witnessed several occasions where somebody died and a specialist in communicating with the departed was summoned to call up the dead man to find out the cause of his death. This reminds me of the fact that this type of practice is not uncommon to the scripture. In I Samuel 28, Saul summoned the witch of Endor to raise prophet Samuel. Samuel was raised and King Saul communicated with him. The belief that the departed though constantly led to continuous sacrificial and prayer practices to the ancestors. Again, this reminds me of several times when my mother carried pounded yams, cola, palm oil, and salt to put on top of my father's grave. She offered prayer, pleading that y father shall please remember to keep watching over us momentarily. In fact, among the Yoruba and Edo people of Nigeria, there existed ancestral festivals, which have become very important festivals. Professor Idowu's stateent that, m "it is only those who have offspring and become old before their departure who become ancestors"[26] is worth close examination. No doubt, it is true that only good and important people who have offspring b become ancestors, however, it does not matter whether one grows old or not. Several people with offspring who died young were venerated as ancestors. In Idah, Benue State, Nigeria, a statue of a young woman who offered herself as a sacrifice for the people of the town to enjoy peace, is still venerated as ancestor till this day. This young woman was given such importance after her death because during a devastating intertribal war, one of the gods requested a human sacrifice for the deliverance of the whole people. She offered herself to be sacrificed to this god. It is also true that some who were heroes who were not necessarily old also became ancestors.

Belief in Spirits

Spirits, according to African belief, are "apparitional entities" which are of a different category of being that I have already discussed above as divinities. Though these spirits are anthropomorphic ally conceived as if they are abstract beings, they are capable of becoming whatever they want to become. Sometimes they may become an object; sometimes they become human beings who are able to melt into vapor. It is also generally believed that all things and places have spirits of their own. Trees, rocks, mountains, hills, forests, and rivers have spirits. These spirits are nameless beings even though they are often identified with certain objects, which they inhabit. However, as nameless as they may be, they certainly have categories by which they can be described.

The first category can be called ghost-spirits. These are the spirit of the departed who wander about. They generally believe that someone who died and was not given a proper burial or not buried at all or someone who was exceptionally and notably wicked and died a bad death will never enter the abode of the wicked but his spirit will wander about on earth.

The second category of spirits is spirits that are "born- to-die." The Yoruba and Ibo people of Nigeria call this category *abiku* and *Ogbanje*, respectively. These are the sadistic spirits who wander about and eventually enter women's wombs and are born as "children to die."

No matter the degree of medical attention, they would die. They are here to torture mothers and fathers. Because of this, pregnant women are constantly advised not to be walking about at certain times of the day or night- mostly midnight and noon. The third category of spirits is spirits that are also painfully real to Africans. They are terribly disastrous and are greatly feared because they can do harm to any person, anywhere, at any time. They usually have their meetings at midnight in the open places or in the bushes. There is a belief that they can reach anywhere in a twinkling of an eye." Their food is to suck the blood of the victim. These disastrous spirits are spirits of witches. Though foreigners may find it difficult to understand it is an indisputable fact that they are real to Africans. Without doubt, to an African of every category, witchcraft is an urgent reality. The fourth important category that is worth mentioning is the guardian spirits. They are important spirits that are inseparable from individual destiny. They are said to determine what the future of the individual holds on earth. If one is fortunate, such fortune is attributed to one's guardian spirit. If a person had a bad luck, such luck is attributed to one's guardian spirit. The Yoruba and Ibo people of Nigeria call it *Ori* and *Chi* respectively. It is not uncommon for Yoruba men and women on arriving at the scene of fatal accident would put their hands on their heads, jump up, tap their foot on the ground and shout, *"ori mi o,"* that is, my head. In other words, they are attributing the bad incident to her guardian spirit.

Another spirit that we may comfortably call the fifth category is can be called diviner spirits. It is generally believed in Africa indigenous religion that spirits when in the process of divination always possesses diviners. Thus, these diviners were said to be taught medicine and a special way of diagnosing and healing patients. The belief in these spirits permeates the life of the average African and as such, is to be taken seriously.

Besides the primordial beings that have been discussed above as divinities, there are number of spirits which are associated with natural phenomena like the earth, rivers, mountains, trees and wind. The earth is venerated because it is believed that spirits inhabits it. Great importance is attached to the earth not only because spirits inhabits it, but also because the earth was spread on the face of the deep and land appeared. Moreover, Obatala used clay from the earth to mould mankind before Olodumare gave breath. When human being dies, it is burried in the earth. Most Africans depend on agricultural materials grown on land to survive.

Since the earth is so useful, there must be some spirits inhabiting it. As there are spirits dwelling on the earth, so are spirits dwelling on rivers, lagoons, and the seas. That is why according to Yoruba belief; Yemoja is the goddes of waters. *Oya* is the goddess of River Niger. Olokun is the lord of the sea. Mountains and hills are not exempted from being inhabited by spirits. It is believed that rocks never die and therefore, if they serve the spirits that live in hills and mountains they will live long. Spirits inhabits not all trees. *Iroko* trees (chlorophora exelsa) are believed to be sacred trees. Other trees include *Eegun* (silk cotton tree called eriodendron orintale), *Ayan* tree (African satiwood) and *Omo* (cordial millenii). Most of these trees are big trees covering other trees. Such trees are venerated because of the belief that spirits live in them. They are considered special trees.

Religious Heritage

Wind are also sacred because spirit live in the wind. Spirits in wind travel invisibly. Oro spirit are believed to be a very dangerous wind because if one is unfortunate and meet such spirit, such a person will be paralyzed. *Aaja* or *Ajija* wind is a spirit traveling by whirlwind and is capable of carrying human being to the forest to instruct such a person in medical science for cure of diseases. Most of the Yoruba priests(*babalawo*) claimed to have been carried away by the *Aaja* wind to be instructed by the spirit.

It must be understood that despite the fact that these divinities are in the constant actions, it is believed by the Yorubas that Olodumare, the Supreme Being is the co-ordinator of the activities and actions of the divinities. Without Him, divinities, spirits have no power and being.

Belief in Mysterious Powers

Mysterious powers that are not explicable how they work. These powers are mystical, esoteric and preternatural powers that are not opened to every person. They are hidden powers that the user must learn and know how to tap them. On some years back when foreign investigators who could not understand these powers in the light of their scientific criteria called they mumbo-jombo or superstitious belief. However, belief in mysterious powers is real and no Africans who lived African traditional society will deny the existence of such powers. These powers that can alter the course of nature also are real and prevalent among the Yoruba people of Nigeria.

Tapping these mysterious powers involved the use of medicine and potent words. Potents words are words that are chanted or uttered purporting to have special powers to change the course of nature. Sometimes, these potent words go hand in hand with the use of medicine. Another time, it is the mere chanting or uttering of the prescribed word in a prescribed formula. Sometimes the potent words involved the performance of some prescribed action or rituals. Some of the medicinal preparation that involved the use of potents words is rings (*oruka*), amulet (*ifunpa*), girdle (*igbadi*), small gourd (*ado*) or needle (*abere*). Among the Yoruba people of Nigeria, such potent words have been uttered by people who know how to utter them. They have been uttered for blessing and for curse. They have been uttered to escape death, to vanish in the approach of imminent dangers, to escape ghastly accident, to destroy the power of enemies or wirld beast, to destroy thieves, and to shorten distance journey. Professor

Religious Heritage

Awolalu gave example of practical occasion when potent words have been uttered to achieve some good and bad purposes among the Yoruba people of Nigeria.

Many of us who have lived among the Yoruba society, heard stories told by the elders about how long distant journey can be shortened. This happened in those days when there were no bicycle or motor vehicle, planes and others to travel in. Elders claimed that by the use of potent words and medicine they used to shorten distances particularly in the moments of extreme anxiety and need. As mentioned above, this kind of medicine and potent words is called, *kanako*, which literally means shorten road or what shortens road. Elders and hunters and soldier tell stories about the use of *Egbe*. Some of us were told about men who are capable of disappearing from imminent danger and finding themselves in any place where they wanted by chanting some potent words. Many are said to have escaped death through this means. Another important medicine and potent words is called *Gbetu gbetu*. It contains an enchanted small gourd covered with red and white clothe which one keeps in the pocket or hand around the neck. At point of an enemy attack, the owner utters some potent words to dismiss the enemy. It is believed that the potent words are capable making the enemy does whatever, the owner of the gourd says. It the owner commands that the enemy runs to the bush, or clear out the way or begin to fight one another, it will certainly happen. Many politicians used this means during the Nigerian political upheavals when organized thurggery was the order of the day.

Telling the history of Old Oyo kingdom, a popular story was told of a bitter encounter between Gbonka Ebiri and Timi, the two war lords against Sango. We were told that Sango, the Alaafin of Oyo set Gbonka Ebiri and Timi against one another by using gbetu gbetu; until one got rid the other that is Gbonka got rid of Timi. When Sango and Gbonka met for a fight, we were told that series of potent words were exchanged. Gbonka use the following potent words to defeat Timi:[27]

Ewe ti a ba ja lowo otun	Leaves picked from the right side,
Otun niigbe,	Are usually kept in the right hand;
Ewe ti a ba ja lowo osi	Leaves picked from the left side;
Osi niigbe	Are usually kept in the left hand;
A-sun-fon fon nitigi aja	A supporting beam usually lies still;
Iwo, Timi! sisun ni koosun	You, Timi, lie still and sleep!

It was told that as a result of this potent words, Timi was overpowered. There is another good illustration of using potent words and medicine together to achieve success. This illustration was given by Babalawo who is an Ifa priest. He claimed that if a person is desperately in search of a job, some herbal preparation and potent words could be used to get job quickly when used as directed. The following potent words will be uttered with the preparation:[28]

E ba mi wase	Help me look for a job
E foro mi lo	Tell my problem to others;
E feti keti	Whisper to every ear
E foro mi lo	And proclaim my need
Bi alantakun ile ba tawu,	When the home-spider makes his web
A fi logi ile	He reports to the wood in the house
E bami wase	Help me look for a job;
E foro mi lo;	Tell my problem to others
E feti keti	Whisper to every ear
E foro mi lo	And proclaim my need;
Bi alantakun oko ba tawu	When the rural spider makes his web
A fi logi igbo	He reports to the forest-wood
E ba mi wase	Help me look for a job
E foro mi lo	Tell my problem to others
E feti keti	Whisper to every ear
E foro mi lo	And proclaim my need
Enu okere lokere fi pode	With the squirrel's own squeaking he invites the hunter
Ti fi ipa a,	That kills him;
Enu yin ni ki e fi ba mi wase	People themselves should use influences
Ti n maa se	To get me a job

Professor Awolalu also reported an incident that took place many years ago when there was a clash between one of the African Indigenous Churches (Aladura Church) and the priests of the traditional religion during Iwo festival in Ilu Titun, Okitipupa Local Government of Ondy State, Nigeria. Iwo Festival was celebrated to honor the river spirits in the area.

These spirits is believed to travel by strong wind. Whoever, stands by its way will be lamed. During this festival everybody sat at home, except the Aladura people who wanted to defile the festival. On this particular day, they decided to have an open-air service procession in defiance of the festival spirit. A disastrous report was given. Many of the members of the Aladura Churches died instantly while others were paralyzed by the wind. It was believed that the mysterious power of this river spirit caused it as the priests of this Iwo Festival carried medicine in their bodies and equipped themselves with potent words uttered against the members of Aladura Churches that caused the destruction. Occasions like these are not unusual in Africa.

African American Biblical Heritage

African American Ancestors in the Old Testament

The African American ancestors were referred to in the Old Testament as Cushites. The existence of the Cushites is the existence of the Egyptians as the existence of Egyptians means the existence of the Cushites. The Cushite was the main military police in Egypt.[29] The Egyptians themselves recorded that the Cushites were their ancestors and that the place where Egyptians are staying was originally water. When the sea rescinded the Cushite ancestors went to that portion of the dry land to colonize it.[30] Egypt is the corridor from where other Africans, south of the Sahara, traveled outside the known world. A closer look at the map of Africa shows that the continent was surrounded by sea-south, north, east, and west. The Cushier gold and other minerals went out to the ancient known world through Egypt. That was the only place where the Cushite could travel by land to the ancient known world. This means that the Eurocentric propaganda that Egypt had no interaction with the so-called Africa, south of the Sahara, is part of the conspiracy to separate Egypt from the rest of Africa by making Egypt part of Europe. In fact, whenever the Cushite came out through Egypt, the ancient known world always call them Cushites and Egyptians simply because it is difficult to differentiate and separate the two.[31] A very good illustration of this problem is the habit of calling all the people who came from South America to North America, Mexicans, even though they are from different countries other than Mexico. The survey of Cushite activities that will be discussed below is closely interwoven with that of Egypt. The survey will be some representative passages in the Old Testament, and will emphasize the process of de-Africanization of the Bible by the Eurocentric scholars.

The Cushit Wife of Moses (Num. 12:1)
The book of Numbers 12:1 recorded the incident of the challenge of Moses' leadership by Miriam when he (Moses) married a *Cushit* woman. Some Eurocentric scholars denied the passage above involving as authentic.[32] Scholars such as Ibn Ezra, J.J Owen, Elliot Binns, and Martin Noth identify the woman with Zipporah, the Midianite.[33] A close examination of the passage shows that the *Cushit* woman was one of the nameless women in the Bible, but was identified by the color of her skin and ethnic origin. Comparison of this passage with other passages where the word *Cushi* and Cushit occur, shows that this woman cannot be a Midianite:

1. The passage does not make any attempt to associate the Cushite woman with Zipporah or a Midianite.
2. That passage will not make sense if *Cushit* refers to Zipporah or a Midianite since Moses had married Zipporah forty (40) years ago because this event took place in the wilderness. Will it make sense for Miriam to get annoyed against Moses for the wife he had married forty years ago? Absolutely no.
3. Midian and Zipporah were never referred to as *Cush* in any biblical record. Midian and Cushite were never used interchangeably.
4. Up to this present time, the word, *Cush* in modern Hebrew means black. The original home of the black is Africa.

The Cushi Military man in King David's Royal Army (II Sam. 18:21,31)

The majority of Eurocentric scholars have no problem identifying the *Cushi*. They agree that he is of African descent. The problem is that since he is of African descent, he must be a slave, serving in David's army.[34] Others say that he is a mercenary from Africa. The truth is that, the Cushite cannot be a slave because if he were a slave, he would have not been the one sent to the King. During a crisis at the battlefront, only a very high-ranking military officer will be sent to report such calamity to the king or president. The Eurocentric idea that the *Cushi* must be a slave or a mercenary does not make sense and is, therefore, untenable. It appears that the only reason why they think he is of African descent is because he performs a function of being a messenger. It has no basis.

Ebed-Melech, the Cushite Delivered the Prophet Jeremiah(Jer. 38:7-13).

Eurocentric scholars do not have any problem identifying Ebed-Melech as having African ancestry, but his position in the court of Zedekiah is disputed. Ebed-Melech, the Cushite was also described as (*saris*). Since the word *saris* could mean eunuch, Eurocentric scholars contend that Ebed-Melech must be a eunuch from Africa. This type of interpretation is based on racial prejudice of the interpreters. This word occurs about forty-five times in the Old Testament and in most cases does not mean eunuch since a eunuch is not permitted in the congregation of Israel. The truth is that the Hebrew word *saris* as used in the Old Testament could also mean "officer," "prince," "commander of the army," or "he who is at the head of the king," or "he goes before the king, one of his confidential advisors."[35] Despite all these various meanings of the word *saris* in the Old Testament, these scholars prefer to see Ebed-Melech as a eunuch instead of the officer or adviser of the king since, to them nothing good comes from Africa. I maintained the word, *saris* here means officer or adviser.

Africa and Africans in the New Testament.

Africa as Place of Refuge For the Infant Jesus (Matt. 2:13-19).

After Jesus was born and angel appeared to Joseph in a dream to take the mother and the child to Egypt-Africa for safety in order to escape Herod's persecution. In obedience Joseph, Mary, and the infant Jesus went to Egypt and remained there until the death of Herod. When Herod had discovered the Magi deceived him he ordered that all the children in Bethlehem and its vicinity be murdered. All the male children in Bethlehem were killed. After the death of Herod, an angel appeared again to Joseph to take the family back to the land of Israel. They lived in Nazareth in the district of Galilee instead of returning to Judea.

For readers to fully understand and appreciate this passage it is

Religious Heritage

important to first of all understand the place of Africa as a place of refuge during the biblical history. Right from the time of Abraham, Africa has been a place of refuge. Genesis 12 recorded the fact that when there was famine in the land, Abraham and his family went to Africa for safety.

Another important instance in which Africa became a haven of safety to the Hebrews was the time of Joseph and Jacob. God made it possible for Joseph to be sold to Egypt so that he could eventually delivered his own people (43:1). Joseph's brothers sold him away because of their jealousy. Joseph was put in charge of the affairs of Egypt. He was given an Egyptian Asenath, the daughter of Portipharah, and the very priest of on for marriage (Gen.41: 45). God was with Joseph to the extent that he became the governor in charge the affairs of Egypt. When there was great famine in the land, Jacob and his family, about seventy of them, went to Egypt at the demand of his son, Joseph, so that they could survive. In Genesis 46:2- 4 the Yahweh assured Jacob that He would be with him in Egypt and that He will make him a great nation. Jacob's family who came to Egypt was seventy souls (Gen.46: 47). The Hebrews went Africa and settled in Goshen (43:11-12) for 430 years before leaving for Canaan when the Pharaoh that knew not Joseph came to the throne. Perhaps, the Hebrews would have not survived without deliverance from Egypt.

Jeroboam rebelled against his father, King Solomon, and he ran for his dear life to Africa, namely Egypt. He served for sixteen years in the Egyptian court until the death of his father (I Kgs.11: 40). While in Egypt he married the queen's daughter, Ano, the sister of Tahpenes. He had a son called Avia from this marriage.36 The marriage to the Egyptian's sister and the long residence in Africa was a diplomatic act. The reason is that it has a very strong influence on his life when he returned to Israel to rule the Nothern Kingdom.

During the destruction of the Northern Kingdom by the Assyrians, many of the Samaritans flee to Egypt for refuge.

The Southern Kingdom (Judah) was destroyed by the Babylonians in 586 BCE. Zedekiah revolted against the Babylonians and Jerusalem was destroyed. After the destruction of Jerusalem, Gedaliah was chosen as a governor of Jerusalem to run the city. But fanatical Jews assassinated him. Fearing that he would come and revenge, they took the Prophet Jeremiah along with them and ran to Africa (Egypt) for safety.

The truth is that from time immemorial Africa has been a place of refuge for the Hebrews and other people. The author of Matthew is aware of this long history and the role of Africa and Africans as being a blessing to the people of God.

However, the main theological implication of the story of the infant Jesus coming to Egypt for safety is that the author wants to draw the readers' attention to the refugee status of Jesus. This is the beginning of his humiliation and exemplary life of humiliation He wants to teach us.

All of these serve as the basis for forbidding the oppression of an alien in the covenant community. The Bible says, " You shall not oppress an alien; you yourselves known how it feels to be an alien, because you were aliens in the land of Egypt" (Ex.23: 9). The fact is that Israel is very conscious of its experience of bondage in Egypt. This consciousness in Israel, like the consciousness of the colonized people of the third world people today, particularly, Africans, colors "the ethos of Israel as revealed in the Old Testament are pervasively than is often realized."

Simon of Syrene, The Compassionate African (Mark 15:21; Matt. 27:32;Luke 23:26)

Pilate released Barabbas, the murderer, to the people instead of the innocent Jesus. After the soldiers have mocked him He was sent to be crucified on the cross of Calvary. On the way to Golgotha, a certain man call Simon from the country of Cyrene was forced by the Romans to help Jesus carry the cross. According to tradition a condemned prisoner were supposed to carry her own cross to the place of his or her execution. It is not normal for the soldiers to show mercy for the condemned prisoner by forcing another person to help him carry the cross. It appears, according to tradition, that Jesus was already carrying the cross and was dragging it on the ground because he was tired. It is also likely that the executioner prefer to crucify him alive rather than have him dead on the way and therefore crucify a dead person on the cross. In such a case they drafted someone to help instead of having to carry the cross themselves.[37] Jesus had been up all night without food, had been cruelly beaten by the soldiers. In such a weakened state, he fell beneath the heavy cross.

Simon of Cyrene must have become a Christian after his experience in Golgota. I believe that Simon, after fulfilling his orders to carry the cross when the disciples have left Jesus, he probably stood nearby to see with his own eyes what happened to Jesus. He also asked about the background of the man who was beaten and crucified because he did not look like a criminal. As he watched him nailed on the cross, in hearing him praying for His tormentors, he probably came to the conclusion that this man must be truly the Son of God. That probably made Him kept in touch with the disciples of Jesus and learnt more about his birth, work, suffering, death and resurrection. He perhaps remains one of the outstanding Christians.

Cyrene roughly corresponds with the present Libya in North Africa. The reference to Simon of Cyrene and the name of his children shows that he was probably well known to the Gospel writers. Mark mentioning these sons of Simon might also be a way of providing some reliable witness to the crucifixion and the remarkable role that an African person has played.[38]

The Ethiopian Eunuch - African Minister of Finance (Acts. 8:26:-40).

In Acts 8:26-40 there is a reference to the so-called "Ethiopian Eunuch." The translation of the Greek word *Eathiop* is misleading. Since that word does not necessarily refer to the present modern Ethiopian country but to the land occupied by the black people, the word should have been translated "African" or "black." Another reason is that the word Ethiopia during the classical period extended more that the modern country of Ethiopia, which the colonial masters, carved during the scramble and the partition of Africa as Ethiopia. At the same time the word "eunuch" is also mistranslated. In most places in the Old Testament and in the LXX, it means "officer" rather than a castrated person. The Greek word *eunoukos* and *saris* mean a very high officer. This is especially true of this man because there is further explanation that he was a financial officer. Haechen is definitely right when he says that eunoukos of LXX, like both eunoukos and *saris* elsewhere, frequently denotes high political or military officers; it does not necessarily indicate castration."[39]

This narrative emphasized two main things: he was an Ethiopian and a eunuch. His name was not given. Instead of that he was introduced into the narrative five times without the clue whether he was a Gentile or Jew. In this narrative Luke wanted to show that the Gospel is also for the peoples who dwell on the outermost fringes of the inhabited world. As an African, and a high officer, he has come to the brightness of the light of Christianity. As example of "not my people who became "my people."

One important thing that must be noticed is how receptive the Ethiopian officer throughout the period. His hospitality was demonstrated in his invitation of Philip to join him and travel with him in his chariot (8.31). As they traveled together and the Ethiopian learns the truth he submitted to baptism. This hospitality is based on the usual generosity of the Africans. Apart from that the Holy Spirit is in control of the whole affairs as evident in this generosity and the submission to baptism by the African.

I find it remarkable that of all the foreigners who were probably involved in this pilgrimage, the only person picked was a black /African from a far away land. Perhaps, Luke picked him and singled him out instead of another foreigner, as a result of not only the importance attached to the Africans in the Old Testament and the Greco-Roman proverbial ranking of the Africans as wealthy, wise and militarily mighty.

Who is this Candace? Or who was the Ethiopian Eunuch? The majority of scholars have associated this Candace with the queen of Ethiopians in the Kingdom of Meroe. One fact is that many queens by the name Candace were mentioned from the classical period and other sources. One queen Candace met Alexander.[40] Strabo also mentioned mentioned other Candaces who were taken prisoners by Petronius.[41] Pliny the Elders also mentioned another Candace that the expedition sent by Nero to explore Ethiopia reported about one queen Candace. One then asked, to which queen Candace is Acts. 8:27 referring to? There is no doubt the Ethiopian Eunuch baptized by Philip can be associated with a servant of one of the Meoitic queens in Africa, but not necessarily the present country of Ethiopia even though from time immemorial the present Ethiopia has applied it to themselves and of course to the Queen of Sheba. The fact is that the term has been used to refer to the farthest of mankind. They live in a place where the sun sets. As discussed earlier, it literally means "burnt-faced," referring the black people and their Diaspora, including the present nation of Ethiopia but not limited to it.

This story shows that the Bible has had a place in the lives of Africans ever since its existence as a body of sacred writings to the present day. Even before the Old Testament reached its final stage as the scripture of the Christians in about 100 CE, Africans were already acquainted with it and using it according to the account of Luke that the African returning from worship in Jerusalem was reading the book of Isaiah 53.

The African Prophets and Teachers in Antioch (Acts. 13:1).

Paul and Barnabas left Jerusalem and came to Antioch where they met prophets and Teachers in the church in Antioch. Among these prophets and teachers were outstanding African men call Simeon called Niger and

Religious Heritage

Lucius of Cyrene. Others are Barnabas, Paul and Manaen. Luke recorded that while they were worshipping together, fasting, and praying, the Holy Spirit said to them, "Separate me Barnabas and Saul for the work whereunto I have called them. And when they have fasted and prayed and laid thier hands on them they sent them away"(13:2-3).

In the previous chapter where I had discussed about an African who carried the cross of Jesus, I mentioned that his name was Simon and his sons names were Alexander and Rufus (Mark 15:21).

It is remarkable that these Africans participated in setting Paul and Barnabas apart for the work of the ministry by laying hand on them. That means they were ordained for the mission to the Gentiles. These prophets and teachers, which include Africans, were able to ordain Paul and Barnabas because prophets and teachers were very important offices in the early church (see Acts 11:27; 1 Cor. 12:18; Eph. 4:11). Surely, if Paul were to become apostle to Gentiles, he would not mind that African Gentile Christians with their zeal and enthusiasm lay their hands on him. This is also one of the evidences that prejudice against black African Christian was absent in the early church. The prejudice and oppression against the black Christian was a modern one and it is unbiblical.

It is important to note the fact that Symeon called Niger and Lucius from Cyrene in Africa are referred to as teachers and prophets is remarkable. Just as Teachers and prophets are not taking lightly in the Old Testament, they are equally important in the New Testament. It is therefore remarkable that there are African prophets and teachers in Antioch.

It is important to examine the wise men in Matthew 2, Stephen in Acts 6-7, the Pentecost in Acts 2, Lydia in Acts 16, Apollos of Alexandria in Acts 18 and Romans 16 concerning their Africanness.

---

[1] E.F. Frazier, *The Negro Church in America* (New York: Shocken Brooks, 1966), 35-61.
[2] Ibid., 33
[3] Ibid. 355-51
[4] Ibid.
[5] *Ebony Magazine*, August 1984, 158.
[6] "The Black Church was Born in Response to Slavery," *Black Church Looks at the Bicentennial- A Minority Report* (Elgin, Illinois: Progressive House, 1976), Crisis vol. 89, Nov. 1982, 27.
[7] *Ebony Magazine*, August 1984.
[8] Eric Lincoln, in Grayraud S Wilmore, *Black Religion and Black Radicalism*, vii

⁹Dr. Ifeanyi enkiti, " Person and Comunity in African Traditional Thought," edited by R.A Wright, African *Philosophy: An Introduction* (Washington: University Press of America, 1979), 165.

¹⁰John S. Mbiti, *Introduction to African Religion* (New York: Praeger Publishers, 1975), 13.

¹¹Alfered B Pasteur and Ivory L, Toldson, *Roots of Souls* (Garden City, NY: Anchor Press, 1982), 112.

¹²J. Akin Omoyajowo, *Cheribum and Seraphim* (New York: Nok Publishers International, 1982),164-165.

¹³Frazier, *The Negro Church in America*, 1-2

¹⁴J.O Awolalu, *Yoruba Beliefs and Sacrificial Rites* (London: Longman Group Limited, 1979), 111-112.

¹⁵Olori-Awo or Oba Awo, which literally means the head of the priests.

¹⁶Gayraud Willmore, *Black Religion and Black Radicalism*, 19.

¹⁷Edward P. Wimberly, *Pastoral Care in the Black Church* (Nashville: Abingdon Press, 1979), 36.

¹⁸Ibid. 35.

¹⁹Ibid.136.

²⁰Wimberly, *Pastoral Care in the Black Church*, 36.

²¹W.E.B DuBois cited by John Brown Childs, *The Political Black Minister: A Study in Afro-American Politics and Religion* (Boston: Hall 1980).

²²

²³Martin Luther King Jr., "The Prophetic Ministry?" *Newsweek*, 20, August 1962, 79.

²⁴ Kofi Asare Opoku, *West African Traditional Religion* (Accra, Ghana: Fep International Private Ltd., 1978), 14-18

²⁵Awolalu, *Yoruba Belief and Sacrificial Rites.*, 53.

²⁶E.B Idowu, *African Traditional Religion: A Definition*, 187.

²⁷Awolalu, *Yoruba Belief*, 70-71

²⁸Ibd.

²⁹Ibid.

³⁰E.A Wallis Budge, *The Egyptian Sudan*, vol. 2, 415-16.

³¹The Hebrews, the Assyrians and the Babylonians, the Greeks see them as such. That is why some times the mentioned them together most of the time.

³²W. Coats, Martin Noth, V.Fritz and W. Rudolph are among the Eurocentric scholars who treat such passage as supplementary. For summary of the discussion, see *Africa and Africans in the Old Testament*, 67-69.

³³See Adamo, *Africa and Africans in the Old Testament*, 69

³⁴William Mckane, *I & II Samuel* (London: SCM Press, 1963), 37-60; Peter R. Ackroyd, *The Second Book of Samuel* (Cambridge: Cambridge University Press, 1977), 172; Ben F Philbeck, Jr., *The Broadman Bible Commentary I Samuel-Nehemiah*, edited by C.J. Allen, Vol. 3, (Nashville: Broadman Press, 1970), 129; Edward Ullendorf, *Ethiopia and the Bible* (Oxford: OUP.1968), Charles Copher, "Egypt and Ethiopia in the Old Testament," in the *Nile Valley Civilizations* (New Brunswick: Transation Periodical Consortium, 1985), 173; Henry Smith, *The Books of Samuel: International Crititical Commentary* (Edinburgh: T & T Clark, 1910), 359.

³⁵ibid. 114-115.

36It is difficult to identify *these* names. However, the name Ano appeared as Anna in he Latin version and can be found in many corpuses of no Egyptian sources with any name of Taphpenes as queen or princess. See Pnina Galpaz, " The Reign of Jerobiam and the Extent of Egyptian Influence," *Biblische Notizen 60* (1991), 13-19.

[37] Craig S. Keener, *Matthew*, 387.

[38] Pheme Perkins, *The New Interpreters' Bible* Vol. VIII (Nashvile: Abingdon Press, 1995), 722.

[39] Ernst Haenchen, *Acts of the Apostles A Commentary* (Philadelphia: Westminster Press, 1965), 310.

[40] *Peudo-Callisthenes*, III.18. See also Edward Ullendorff, "Candace (Acts VIII.27) and the Queen of Sheba" Journal of New Testament Studies 2 (1956), 53-56.

[41] Strabo, XVII, 820. See also E. Ullendorff, 53.

CHAPTER FOUR

AFRICAN AMERICAN CULTURAL HERITAGE

Music

As said earlier in my introduction, there is no clear-cut division between the historical, religious and cultural heritage and that the division is for the sake of simplicity and understanding. This is especially true in the case of chapters three and four. The most obvious example is the section on musical heritage in chapter four. It could also be classified as religious heritage, but music is very broad and could be religious or secular.

This chapter deals with music, the concept of time, and name giving. As I discuss these, I would also like to remind my readers that although these things are visible everywhere among the African American people, there are always exceptions due to the influence of western life-style.

Songs

Songs of the African American Ancestors (Africa)

Songs are important part of life's activities in Africa. Themes and content of songs are determined according to certain events and matters of interest to the community. Dr. Ashenafi Kebede classified African songs into two main categories - sacred and secular. However, he admits the fact that there is some songs of mixed types, which are difficult to be, classified as either strictly sacred or secular.[1] Here, our classification though not strictly technical, will be according to functions simply because of this mixed character of many songs. It will be similar to the type of classification of drums that will be discussed later.

In Africa, there are numerous types of songs with different functions. While some of these songs are sometimes restricted to a particular occasion, others are used generally. These types of songs include royal songs, work songs, burial or funeral songs,

Cultural Heritage

war songs, hunting songs, instructional songs, social commentary songs, and others.

In most cases, the royal songs are sung exclusively for Kings and Chiefs, mostly during an installation ceremony or other occasions when a Chief or a King performs some heroic deeds. These royal songs may be sacred or secular, or purely ceremonial. They may be sung at the time when a king performs some religious ceremonies, like making elaborate sacrifices to the gods of the village, or to his own household
gods. These royal songs may be historical, or cradle in nature, but usually
to praise the King and the gods who are believed to have installed him. These royal songs sometimes function as a means of communication. An
example of this is when the King has an announcement to make to his subjects or to the community. Usually before the announcement, the royal song may be sung or chanted.

Work songs appear to be one of the most common songs in Africa. These songs are sung when cultivating a field, when harvesting crops, when fishing, when babysitting, when grinding corn or beans, while washing dishes, when weaving clothing, and all kinds of work. This type of song may be historical (narrating the heroic deeds of his great-great-grandfathers) or cradles (calling the worker various names) in their contents. African people believe that these songs appeal to the emotion of the workers and thereby strengthen their spirits to work harder and faster.

This reminds me of several events in my village (Irunda Isanlu) Kogi State, Nigeria. The young men are formed into age groups. Sometimes these groups may be twenty or twenty-five, or even thirty. They chose a certain day of the week when all of this age group went to one of the members' farms to harvest or to cultivate his field. This was rotated until they went to every member's farm. Among this group, a leader called *Soje* and a singer were chosen. I remember that one Wednesday morning in 1963, this group came to my brother's farm. The singer sang to each of the members who cultivated my brother's farm. However, they sang more to *Soje*, who was supposed to have cultivated more of the field than any of the members. I was so glad, not only that they would finish cultivating my brother's farm, but also mainly because plenty of food would be available.

Burial or funeral songs are songs that are peculiar to that time when someone of importance dies. These songs may be sacred or secular, but mostly sacred. These types of songs may be sung while digging a grave, or the next day after the burial (*ite*), or seven days after the deceased has died. The songs on the seventh day of the burial are usually sung by women, relatives and wives of the deceased among Yagba people, Kogi State, Nigeria. This is the funeral dirge sung at the grave of the deceased for seven days. The funeral, or burial songs are songs sung to communicate and appease the spirit of the deceased for the purpose of maintaining harmony with the dead and the living. *Ite* songs are elaborately ceremonial and the dead is lavishly entertained with dances, food and drink.

War songs are songs used to sound an alarm for an emergency occasion. They serve as a medium of communication to tell the public that the state of war exists and that the elders and the strong men need to be ready. They warn the women to stay under their roofs.

Hunting songs are sometimes like the war and work songs. The hunting song communicates to the community that it is time to gather bows and arrows and guns to go hunting. It serves also to stimulate the interest of the men, who previously were not willing to go hunting, to get up and go. A hunting song can be either religious or secular, but most of the time they are religious. The hunting songs are sung also when a hunter kills big and ferocious animals and during the worship of the gods.

Among the Yoruba people of Nigeria, the hunting songs are sometimes sung in praise of Gun (god of iron), who is believed to have helped them to be successful.

Instrumental songs may be a form of telling stories; they may be fictional or completely poetic. The content instructs the public, usually children, pregnant women and others to be careful of some situations, or actions. It may teach the codes and mores of the society, or correct the unruly behavior. It may be sacred or secular.

In Africa, the styles of songs vary, usually according to the type of songs. The style may be sung by a chorus, usually in African songs with more than nine persons. It may be religious or secular. Another unique structure of songs in Africa is the song sung in the form of voice masking," an imitation of musical instruments.[2] This is accomplished by singing or talking through a musical instrument. Sometimes the voice may be an imitation of birdcalls or mating calls of animals.

Although there are different types of structures in African songs, what appears to be the most popular is the responsorial style of singing. This is done in the form of a call and response manner. The style of this call and response may be an imitational response (the second singer imitates the first), or antiphonal (two performers in each group). The responsorial approach also includes songs in which a single leader and a group response exist.

All that I am trying to say is that songs in Africa are not songs just for pleasure. They have specific structures and functions. Such structures and functions manifest themselves in the African American songs, as we shall see below.

African American Music

For so long, scholars have examined African American history and culture in the context of African past and their findings have supported the premise that the institution of slavery has not either destroyed in anyway the cultural legacy of African slaves or erase the memories of an African past.[3] It is gratifying that even though the African slaves were exposed to Euro-American culture, they resisted the cultural imprisonment imposed on them. "They adapted to life in Americas by retaining a perspective on the past. They survived an oppressive existence by creating new expressive forms out of African traditions, and they brought relevance to Euro-American customs by reshaping them to conform to African aesthetic ideals."[4] Maultsby continues:

> The continuum of an African consciousness in America manifests itself in the evolution of an African American culture. The music, dance, folklore, religion, language, and other expressive forms associated with a culture of slaves were transmitted orally to subsequent generations of American blacks. Consequently, Levine adds, many

aspects of African culture continue 'to exist not as mere vestiges but as dynamic, living, creative parts of group life in the United States.' This proposition contradicts that of earlier scholars who interpreted the fundamentals of African-American culture as distorted imitations of European-American culture.[5]

For more than 150 years, the slavers unwittingly assisted in the preservation of African identity in African American music tradition. They brought African music instrument on board of he slave ships so that the slaves could dance, entertain, and exercise during the long voyage to the New World. Those musical instruments were concrete documents reminding African slaves in America of their cultural heritage.[6]

Generally music is an integral aspect of black community life all over the world. It serves so many functions. Music in African tradition is participatory activity. Music making in African tradition involved the active participation of all those present at the musical event. When the Africans arrived in America, the first song sung was an African song. They carried their love for songs along with them to America. It serves as instrument of unity.

Call Song or Cry Song

When the slaves who worked on the plantation were forbidden to talk to each other, the means by which they communicated with each other was through songs. The "call songs" were employed to deliver short speeches or messages and were converted into songs to attract attention, warn of coming danger, to summon people to work, or to gather. During the early part of slavery, these songs were sung in African dialect. They are African-derived songs. These types of songs are used to gather villages, to send messages, to organize work groups, or a call for food. Up till today, these call songs still exist and are used in some of the African villages.

Work Songs

Work songs existed among the plantation workers. Early in the

Cultural Heritage

time of slavery, the songs of the African slaves in the United States were completely African-derived songs. The desire to sing by the African-Americans on the plantations was welcomed by the slave owners as long as they did their work. As in Africa, where singing accompanied work, the African Americans sang on the plantation. When the slave owners noticed that the slaves worked harder as they sang, they even encouraged songs. Sometimes the slave owners paid those song leaders who directed the song. The subject of the songs, as in Africa, depended on the recent experience of the slaves.

The most popular and probably the finest work song by the African-Americans is "Long John." This song is sung responsorial. Without question, the melodies, the rhythmic characteristics of the song, the vocal style, and the performing mannerisms of the singers are said to be African-derived,[7] but the language is American.

Children Songs

Another distinctive type of African-American song is children song. African American children songs retain much of the numerous elements from African heritage. Most of these songs may be game or educational songs. Sometimes they are diversified according to age, sex, or both, it has been rightly observed that these Black American children songs in their "general approach to performance - the manner or the way the songs were sung, the way the games were played, the vocal quality, the pictures - draw heavily on African roots. Singing antiphonally and responsorial, hand clapping with off-beat syncopation, and body motion, are commonly found in children's play songs of both sub-Saharan African and the African American traditions."[8]

The Blues

The Blues became an important African American song. Generally speaking, blues are divided into four main categories: country blues, racial blues, city blues, and urban blues.[9] Blues are sung to express deep emotion and concern for the African people. The condition of love, sex, and loneliness, suffering in prison, plantation, poverty, and protests are vividly expressed. In the blues, the virtuosity, which is also found in African American sermons, the African Americans regard writings, and riddles as a "carry-over" from Africa.[10] The use of "repetitive singles, doubles, triples, and quadrupling stanzas in songs" is regarded as the characteristics of vocal music of sub-Sahara Africa. The characteristics of African vocal music affects t he texts of the blues. Such Africanism as "tonal glides," "accentuation," "mouth resonance," and "microtonal inflection" of African American English survived in the way the blues are sung and constructed.[11] This results in "unique rhythmic schemes," "rhythmic structures, vocal dynamics," and syllabic ornaments of the African American songs, which make such songs irresistibly appealing to the listeners. It is therefore not uncommon to see in the African American English, "de" for "the," hee" for "here," "goin" for "going," and "aint' for I won't."

African heritage is clearly visible in African-American religious music. Even though the slaves adopted Christianity when they arrived in the United States and abandoned their African Traditional Religion, much Africanism still survives in their religious practices. The social implications of music are still the same in both Africa and African-American cultures. Spirituals are sung in the Church and at home, during ceremonies, working, meetings, baptism, etc. Antiphonal, responsorial. singing, the use of vocal "slides," groaning, moanings and shouting, accompanied with the clapping of hands and dance in Black American Churches, are characteristic of their African heritage. The possession of spirit with body jerks, jumps and convulsions, which are important characteristics of African worship, are not uncommon among the African-American people. Music plays an important role, not only during singing, but also during preaching.

Like the Africans, the African Americans use music to serve life in all its manifestations. Music serves both the living and the dead. No group of people is more affected by music than the Africans and the African-Americans.[12] As in Africa where songs and drums are used as a means of survival and a means of increasing production, the slave singers were paid to sing in order to increase the ability of the African slaves to work harder.

Cultural Heritage

Singing, like dancing, also becomes a therapy and a means of survival. Songs were sung in most places. The ability of the African Americans to bend notes with their voices as they please is due to their African heritage.

This African heritage was carried to the African American Churches, where it manifests itself with some exactness. Music and frenzy characterize the religion of the African Americans. Music then becomes one of the most original and beautiful expressions of human life among the African-American worshippers. Such, of course, cannot be disputed as having its roots in Africa. Even when songs are sung from the regular white Methodist or Baptist hymnals, it is remarkable that the tones are different. They are sung with actions and distinctive tones and melodies that reflect African background. Even when the Western musical instruments are employed, the music they perform is different and distinctively African.

Without denying certain Western influences on some of the African American songs, when the general characteristics of these songs are considered, they are distinctly African. This Africanism is what responsible for the distinctiveness of African American songs. That is why the African American songs are easily recognizable over the radio, even without seeing or knowing who is singing them. The rhythm and tones, especially Church songs, resemble quite clearly songs sung during *imole* and Olokesi worship in my village (Irunda Isanlu, Kogi State, Nigeria). The tones and the rhythm of the African-American songs remind me of when the old people of the Evangelical Churches of West Africa (ECWA) at Egbe, Odo-Ere, Igbaruku and Isanlu sang the ECWA hymns. Whenever I attend the African-American Churches, the songs bring to my memory my past school years, when I had to do my student pastoring in the above villages. It is therefore known beyond any doubt when the African musical heritage appears among the African-Americans. I agree that it may be difficult for those who have never lived among these African people in Nigerian villages to recognize this heritage, but those of us who were born in Africa and have lived and pastored these people can easily recognize the similarity.

Cultural Heritage

Musical Instruments

African American Ancestors

The scientific study of musical instruments (organology) has come to be an important study in this age. It tells about the classification, measurement and descriptions of musical instruments. What shall be our major concern here is the classifications and descriptions of the major types of African musical instruments and some of them that have survived in America. Generally, musicologists classified musical instruments into five main categories: (1) idiophones, (2) chordophones, (3) membranophones, (4) aerophones and electrophones.

The most common of African musical instruments are idiophones. These are the types of instruments which produce sound by vibrating bodies. These instruments are mostly worn on the human body or attached to another instrument. Some are shaken or struck by hands in order to produce sounds. Such that are shaken or struck by human hands are called the primary idiophones. While some may require tuning, others don't. Examples of these types of musical instruments are gongs, Xylophones, bells, cymbals, clappers, Marimbas, metal and gong rattles, shakers and others. They are used very extensively for African music and dance.

Membranophones are also another important type of musical instrument in Africa. These types of musical instruments are drums with animal skin or membrane heads. Almost every society in Africa has drums called by various names and differs in size, shape and material. Some are as tall as ten to fifteen feet, carved from wood. Others are extremely small and made out of wood, pots or kegs. Some of these drums among the Yoruba people of Nigeria are called *dundun* (talking drum); imole (small drum) Eku. Drums play a very important role in both religious and secular ceremonies in Africa. Most are always accompanied by songs and dancing.

Cultural Heritage

Aerophone musical instruments are the type of musical instruments which produce sound when some quantity of air is blown into the pipe. Three types of aerophones are flutes, whistlers, single and double-reed pipes, and horns and trumpets. The most popular of these types of aerophones are flutes, made out of bamboo. They are found almost everywhere in Africa wherever bamboo grows. The single and double-reed aerophones are found mostly in North Africa. Although not very common among the societies in Sub-Sahara Africa, reed aerophones are found in some parts of West African countries such a Ghana, Benin and Chad.

Trumpets and horns are also made of bamboo, elephant tusks animal horns, wood, metal, and other materials. They are also use~ for both secular and religious ceremonies.

Chordophones are string instruments. Although most of these types of instruments are found in the Northern part of Africa, they are also available in the Sub-Sahara region. There are four main classes that are widely recognized: lutes, lyres, zithers and harps. Some of these are made from animal skins and tissues, wood and calabash.

African-American

As stated earlier, the Africans were brought to the Americas as early as the 1600's of the Christian era. By *1803*, half of the population of New Orleans was black. When these people were uprooted from Africa, their musical heritage came with them. This was evident in the fact that as early as *1817* and *1880*, African music styles of instruments were very popular among the African-Americans, especially in New Orleans. These African styles of musical instruments were not imported from Africa, but were made here in America by the African slaves, who were still aware of the native musical instruments. Although the African slaves in the United States were forbidden to play their African-style loud drums, they were able to play African soft sounding music on string instruments; such as they had known in Africa.

Cultural Heritage

Among the chordophones, the most popular of the American style instruments was the "homemade" folk banjo. The banjo musical instrument is not only the most popular; it has the longest existence in the Americas. The European writers documented the existence of this instrument as early as 1700. Thomas Jefferson reported as early as 1783 that the music proper to the Negroes is the "Banjar." These banjo instruments were made of ---half-gourd resonators covered with animal skins" on wood or bamboo with four strings. The strings were made of "guts" or "horse hair" instead of nylon. This type of banjo is still found today in African-Jamaica, Haiti, Cuba and the United States. Other chordophone musical instruments among the African-Americans in the United States include "gut buckets" or "tubs" or "wash tubs." The use of similar instruments like the trumpets and horns were common among the African Americans before the adaptation of the European brass horns and trumpets.

Among the idiophone type of musical instruments were "washboards," used to provide rhythm. They are made of food cans, bottles, rattles, jawbones of horses and other materials.

African drum styles were later used by the African-Americans when performing their African dances (circle dances). These types of drums were later adopted and modernized into the western style.

What is significant is the fact that the Africans who came to the Americas were able to adapt their African musical instruments to their environment. They did not just borrow or leave them in the same condition of the African drums. They were improved on, and the use became extensive
after they were modernized.

Dance

Dance of the African American Ancestors (Africa)

In Chapter Three, I have already discussed the fact that wherever there is music (namely, songs and drums), it automatically produces action. This is due to the fact that African people are sensitive to music. The automatic response to music is dance.

Dance in Africa is a discipline that involves a great physical phenomenon and is culturally patterned. African dance sometimes differs from place to place; however, there is also the same common homogeneity. The style of dance is always patterned after the rhythm of the drum. The style of dance also differs according to sex, age, social status, profession, nationality and ethnic membership." Sometimes dance may serve as a means of differentiating one from another. Dance also is an expression of joy, sorrow, war and peace.

The ritual dances may symbolize ideas, beliefs, activities and profession of the dancers. Ritual dances become part and parcel of the traditional activities of the African societies; it is often accompanied with drums, or other musical instruments, and performed with elaborate ceremonies. In this case, the local priests most of ten are the leaders of these types of ceremonial dances. Those ritual dances are very common among the Yagba people of Nigeria. *Egungun* dances most of the time involve the wearing of masks. Almost all cultic celebrations involve elaborate dance. Among these ritual dances is the "spirit dance." When the deity possesses dancers, they perform frenzied and acrobatic movements.

Wedding dances may he secular or religious, depending on the family of the couple and their religious conviction. They may be performed by both sexes.

Royal dances are performed during the installation of a Chief. They may serve the purpose of enhancing his political authority and his popularity. As there are male dances, there are also female dances. Most often, the female dances are less rigorous than the male dances. Male dances involve much kicking, jumping and leaping on most occasions.

There is what we may call animal dances, which are mostly performed by hunters. Sometimes it reflects the belief of the hunters in totemic worship.

War dances also exist. They are performed before the

battle. However, since inter-tribal wars do not exist nowadays, these war dances are adapted to what we may call dance drama, purely for entertainment.

Abdominal dances are not uncommon in Africa. This is what the modern Europeans call "belly dances." Probably as a result of lack of information about the existence of such dances in Africa from antiquity, they erroneously attributed the origin of these dances to the Arabs. The Arabs first encountered this type of dance in Egypt and later took it over. This is probably the reason why they call this abdominal dance *masri* or "Egytian." Today, such dance is performed and taught in Europe and the Middle East, but it is African in its origin. There exist what we may call "black dances." Such is performed among Yagba people of Kogi State, Nigeria during *egungun*, *ite* and *imole* ceremonies.

In Africa, we also have healing and medicinal dances, and such dances are mostly accompanied by drums. These types of dances are popular among the Wan Yamwezi of Tanzania.

Dance cannot be separated totally from everyday life and religion. A Western observer examines the importance of dance in African Church services and comments:

> African Churches have one form of worship, one Sacrament, which we in the West have barely discovered: dance. All African Churches, those started by missionaries, but now in African hands, and those founded by African prophets and evangelists, share dance. In Catholic, Protestant, and Orthodox Churches dance is an integral part of each Sunday celebration. Dance in Africa embodies thanksgiving to God, to Christ, and to the Holy Spirit. It is a joy to be able to dance before the altar of the Lord, bringing offerings as, an expression of gratitude for God's abundant earthly gift.[13]

African American Dances

I have emphasized above the fact that dance is life in Africa. In other words, dance is not taken lightly, and it is an important aspect of the total life of the Africans. African dances are performed during funerals and other religious ceremonies. They dance at the time of war, at the time of a wedding, at the time of

Cultural Heritage

wrestling and at almost every occasion. This type of approach to life becomes a way of responding to their environment with the greatest simplicity. It becomes a means of survival, a means of communication, and a means of maintaining the unity of life.

When the Africans were brought to America, they could not help but carry their dance to America. The first song and the first dance of the African Americans in the United States are an African song and dance. Dance becomes an indispensable part of life among the African American people in the United States. The African Americans, like the Africans, have a distinctive ability to feel, express feelings creatively and dramatically.[14] Like the Africans, they feel music with body and soul and then transform such feelings into action, superb energy and great emotion.[15] This feeling results into movements, clapping, and tapping of the feet. The African-Americans, like the Africans, have bodies which are alert and lively. They respond spontaneously, and react easily and naturally to all the rhythms of the environment.[16] Singing and dancing, then, become something natural and are the depth of soul, so that wherever the African goes his dance is carried with him. The African American then converts the African dance to what we might call a therapeutic function. It becomes a means of survival and coping with the world of injustice, oppression, segregation, and racism.

This concept of dance is carried to the African-American Churches in America. The preachers present their sermons rhythmically and dramatically, and with some unrestrained behavior. The congregation, then, naturally responds rhythmically and dramatically as people possessed with spirits in Africa. The result is that, the African American Churches become emotional Churches - not just mere emotionalism, but emotion filled with spiritualism, sincerity and enthusiasm.

A close examination of most of the famous distinctive African American dances has persuaded me that they have their counterpart in African dances. A typical example of this is the break dance. This break dance resembles the *Egungun* and hunter dances of the Yagba people of Nigeria. The movement of the legs, the jumping and the rhythmical moving on the floor like a snake, naturally has their foundation in Africa. Whenever I watched the break dance, I cannot help but remember home. The only difference is that it was recreated, refashioned and better organized than the *Egungun* and hunter dances of Yagba people of Nigeria.

It must be said that African American music extends beyond the trait list. It can be viewed in term of "creative process" which allows for continuity and change.

The Concept of Time

As I discussed the concept of time, it is important that some preliminary statement be made for the sake of proper understanding of this section. It is very important that my readers bear in mind as they read this section that there are always exceptions in an individual case. It is also important to remember that people discussed are generally the ordinary public, who are the main bearers of culture. I do not refer to highly sophisticated Africans and African Americans who have been saturated in the Western concept of time. The occasion in which this concept of time is very evident among the Africans and African Americans is mostly during voluntary meetings, Church services, clubs and many voluntary occasions. This generally excludes areas such as jobs and school classes, which are compulsory. In such cases, African and African-Americans have the capability of adjusting to the Western concept of time.

African American Ancestors: Concept of Time

The concept of time in Africa is not a chronological reckoning in a vacuum like the Western concept. Time in Africa is reckoned in terms of events -, which occurred (past), occurring (present), and will occur (future). For time to make sense in Africa it has to relate to something that has been experienced, that is being experienced, or that is to be experienced.[17] This does not mean that Africa does not differentiate between what is time and the event in time. It means that for time to be meaningful, events that take place in time are indispensable. Thus, the African people are more concerned with the simplicity of time in terms of block ideas than what we might call the exactitude of time. Time, therefore is experienced partly in the life of the individual and partly through the community. The reckoning of the day, the month, the year and one's lifetime or entire human history can be meaningful only with specific events. Since time is closely associated with events, how then does one reckon with time in the future? Because of this problem, some scholars have maintained that Africans have no concept of the future.[18]

Although this may be true in some areas where the authors of the idea have immediate knowledge, it is a sweeping generalization to say that such is true of all African countries. 1 know for certain that such is not true among the Yoruba people of Nigeria. The idea that the Yoruba people are conscious of the future is seen in their expressions, such as *Oogorun odun Kii se lailai*, that is, a hundred years is not forever.[19] The Yoruba people are aware and concerned about the future. That is why many people would go to the priests to find out or uncover what events lay in the future, either for themselves or for their children. Divination is the common way of unfolding such future. The fact that in the olden days when the King died, they buried some properties, like jewelry and food, shows that they believed that there is a long future even for the dead. The reason f or burying these materials is that the Yoruba people believe that the dead person has a long journey to travel before reaching his destination. Therefore, they would need some properties to use and some food to eat on the way. In the light of this, it is not appropriate to say that Africans only have the concept of the past, present without the future.

This concept of time affects almost every aspect of African life. It affects it when they attend meetings, Church services or any religious service. The most obvious area where this concept of time can be clearly seen is during Church services. Africans are flexible with time. They try to master time instead of letting time master them. Africans have learned to deal with this time in a very traditional way, which may be difficult f or most Westerners to understand. Because time devoid of events makes little sense in Africa, the exact time they get to meetings is flexible; how long they spend at meetings depends on the importance of this meeting. As complicated as this might seem to the Westerners, Africans learn to relate and understand this concept of time very well. Examples of the way they deal with this is that if a meeting or a

Cultural Heritage

Church meeting is scheduled to begin at 11:00. A.M. sharp, most African people understand this to mean 11:30 A.M. This is because the meeting never starts on the exact time. In fact, people may not arrive at the meeting until 11:30 A.M., despite the fact that the announcer says 11:00 A.M. Although there might be exceptions to this rule, as mentioned earlier, nevertheless this is true in most cases. Everybody seems to feel at home with this concept of time, unless there are those who have been influenced by the Western concept of time. The church services or meetings may last two to three hours, depending on how interesting the service or the meeting is. To the Africans, as long as the meetings or the church service takes place, most of the time the exact time and how long, does not matter very much. In this way, Africans learn to be masters of time and refuse to let time in vacuum control them. In other words, unlike the western people who are slaves to time, Africans are masters of time. When a meeting or Church service becomes interesting and it appears there is not enough time, Africans create or produce time. Those foreign visitors who do not understand this concept always express, "Oh these Africans are always late."[20] Dr. Mbiti expressed this concept of time very beautifully:

In Western technological society, time is a commodity, which must be Utilized, sold and bought; but in traditional African lifetime has to be created or produced. Man is not a slave to time; instead, he 'makes' as much time as he wants.[21]

This is not because there are no watches or clocks in Africa. A person who may have several watches in Africa looks at the watches, but still follows what we may call this African concept of time. Although several so-called "intellectuals" have rejected this African concept of time, the actual reality is there and it happens every day.

African-Americans: Concept of Time

In considering the concept of time among the African-American people, it is important to emphasize that among those who are holding very steadfastly to the African concept of time are the common people, who are the majority. As in Africa, some highly sophisticated African-American people are sometimes exceptional in the attempt to live a western life. I believe that the carriers of

Cultural Heritage

the heritage, both in Africa and in America, are the above people.

During my seven years' observation of the African-American people and their concept of time, there is very little difference from the African concept. The most obvious places where this African concept of time can be seen very clearly are Church services, meetings, and other voluntary activities. The African-American people are flexible. They know how to adapt themselves to every situation. When it comes to things of compulsion, like daily jobs, and other events, which demand being present at an exact time, they have no problem observing that exact time. However, when it comes to the situations and events that are of voluntary nature, this African concept of time can be evident. They seem not to worry about the so-called being 'late" in the western concept of time. While this concept of time is called "African time," among the Africans, it is called---colored people time" (C.P.) among the African-Americans. Most of the African-American Churches have the usual custom of not being slave to the exactitude of time. The Church services in most places never start at the exact time as announced on the bulletin. Although there may be exceptions to this, it is generally true that no one can predict how

long the African-American Churches' services would last. Sometimes it may generally take two or three or even four hours. These services are said to depend on how the "Spirit moves," and how enjoyable the services are. In almost all the places where I have been invited to preach, whenever I asked the pastor how long should I preach, the usual answers have been - how the "Spirit leads." Perhaps it is right to say that this is due not only to African concept of time, but also the African religious heritage of the African-American people. Those who do not understand this African cultural heritage which still influences the African-American people always complain, "Black people are always late." To the African- Americans, like the Africans, the most important thing in their observation of time is the events and not just the chronometer (clock) in vacuum. As long as the events take place and are enjoyable, the African American person is satisfied. The exact time is not important as such. Like the Africans, the African Americans

95

Cultural Heritage

"create" and "produce" time to suite themselves without the pressure of the so-called lateness." This African concept of time is still a factor and a common recognizable element that affects the everyday activities of the African American people. No matter how absurd this heritage sounds to the African-American intellectuals who have totally embraced Western culture; it is a reality among the common people, who are of the majority.

Whenever those of us from Africa encounter the African-Americans behaving in certain ways like us, we always say *"Awon omo Iya wa ni,"* that is (literally), they are our mothers' children. In many words, they behave like us, because we have the same ancestors and the same blood.

Name-Giving

African-American Ancestors

Perhaps my readers would begin to wonder why name-giving is included as part of the African cultural heritage. The reasons for this can be found in the great importance attached to names in Africa as a means of expressing the state of mind of the immediate parents and that of the community. Names may be given as a means of perpetuating one's religion. In Africa a name is not only a means of identifying the individual, it is also a means of expressing the community's contemporary attitude to life. It is also a means of communicating, congratulating, acknowledging and welcoming the newborn to the earth. More importantly, it is a means of maintaining the cultural unity of the society. For these reasons, almost every African name has meaning behind it. Names are given to the newborn with careful scrutiny, and sometimes the priests, who are able through divination to predict the future of the children, are consulted for appropriate names. This is very important, because African-American ancestors believe that the names one gives to his or her children may influence their future behavior and achievement.

Our discussion on names shall be very brief, focusing our attention on the importance of these African names as a means of perpetuating African heritage, we shall also discuss the present state of this cultural heritage among the African American people.

Cultural Heritage

Since several writers have discussed and compiled extensively African names, their meanings and the respective countries of origin. We shall not waste much time in giving a list of names, but will give a few examples, mostly Yoruba names (Nigeria).

Naming children after their paternal or maternal relative is a recognizable thing in Africa, especially in Nigeria. In this system of naming, a child bears the name of his or her grandfather, or grandmother, or his or her immediate father or mother. The main value of this type of naming system is that such names link several generations together, thus bridging the long gap between the grandparents and the grandchildren. It is also a means of perpetuating the names of the ancestors, and a way of honoring them. By giving the grandparent's name, it means that the ancestor never dies. It is also believed that in doing this, a child may automatically inherit his ancestor's god virtues. The above naming system may be due to the fact that Africans generally believe that there could be some special communication between the ancestors who have died, and that such ancestors are watching over the living relatives in order to protect them.

As said earlier, the condition for African names varies. It is mostly a way of expressing the state of mind of the parents. Such names may be compensatory names. By this, I mean that the immediate child who is born after his or her father or mother's death may be named to reflect such condition of mind. Such child may be regarded as a substitute or a compensation for the father or mother's death. It is mostly believed, especially among the Yoruba people of Nigeria, that the dead father has come back in the form of the newborn child to comfort the family, Such child may bear *Ba-ba-tun-de* (male), or simply *Baba* or *I-ya-tunde* (female) - father or mother has come back. If it is believed that such a child is given to comfort the family, then the child may bear *I-tu-nu* (female), meaning comfort or consolation. If such child is a male, he may bear *Ayo* or *A-yoku*, that is, there is still joy.

Names may express wishes, hopes or requests. Such names given to children may be a request for joy or success in life. It may be a way to express what the parent of this child wants him or her to be. Such names among the Yoruba people of Nigeria may be *O-la-bo* - riches has come; *Ba-mi-she* - do it for me; *O-lu-pese* or

Pese or *Olu* - God is the provider; *E-Kun-da-yo* or *Dayo* - my sorrow becomes joy. Such names are believed to belong to the category of invocative names." Such names have special powers and not only can they influence the character of the child, but they can provide or bring some happiness to the homes.

In Africa, names given to a child may be determined by the time or the exact condition of the time in which a child is born. If a child is born at the time when the family was blessed, such child may bear *Ayo* - joy (male or female); *I-bu-Kun* - blessing (female); *Ife* - love (female); *Ola* - riches or honor (male or female) and others. Names in Africa may express gratitudes to God or to the divinities, or to the parents of the newborn. Examples of these names among the Yoruba people of Nigeria are: *Iyin* - praise (male or female), *Mo-du-pe* or *Dupe* - I thank you or thanks (male or female). Children born during the time of the year's festival may be called *Bodunde* - comes with festival.

Names may denote an advice to parents or the community to be patient, to endure or persevere. Or it may reflect the value of patience, endurance and perseverance which the parents have endured in the past years of difficulties and pain. Such a child may be called *Su-ru* - patience (male or female); *Foriti* - endurance (male or female), and others. Such names become a way of communication among the people. Names given to a child may be determined by where he was born. If he is born in a foreign land or in another far-away city, other than home, such a child may bear *Ba-mi-dele*, or simply *Dele* -Come home with me (male or female); *To-Kun-bo* - come from abroad or overseas (male). When a child is born on the road, he is called *A-bi-o-na* - born on the road (male-or female).

Names may also denote times, days and years. Since Yoruba people believe that the days of the week are sacred and each day has its special meanings, children may be named after the day of the week. A child born on Sunday may bear *Bose* or *Ebun*; on Friday he may be called *Jimoh*; and on Monday, *Aje*. Hence, it is not unusual for people to bear Monday, Tuesday, Friday, Saturday, Sunday, Etc.

African names may be dedicatory names. Such names are given as a sign of gratitude and dedication, to God, divinities or

Cultural Heritage

ancestors. Thus, among the Yorubas of Nigeria, there are names such as, *O-luti-mi* or *Timi* God supports me; *O-sa-yo-mi* - *Orisa* divinities deliver me; *Ogun* - god of iron, *Osun* - goddess of the Sea; *O-lorun-le-ke* - God is victorious; *O-lu-se-yi* or *Seyi* - God provides this; *Ba-ba-yo-mi* - father delivers me; *I-ya-gbe-mi* - mother supports me. Among the Yoruba people, as is among other African people, other patterns of naming children include the way the child was delivered, whether the child first sticks his head, or leg or hand out during delivery. Sometimes the behavior of the child may determine the name to be given to the child. African people are so rich in name-giving that we cannot describe all within the scope of this work. All we have done is to give representative examples.

The above discussion has shown the importance of names in Africa. Because of this special importance attached to African names, Africans do not just give any type of names to their children. They do not just bear something like Stone, Black, White and others. This importance attached to names requires, especially among the Yoruba people of Nigeria, elaborate naming ceremonies. Eight days after a male child or seven days after a female is born, the family and the community gather together to celebrate, to drink, dance, sacrifice, pray and welcome the child by giving a name ritualistically. However, the ceremonies associated with naming a child differ from one country to another. But it serves as a time of praise, gratitude and rejoicing. One of the greatest values of these African names is that a name given to an individual may reveal the environment or identify him with his locality. Thus, by knowing individual names, one is able to know either from which locality, state or country one comes. African names, as a means of communicating the identity of the tribe from which one comes and generally as a means of maintaining African culture, can he very valuable to the African Diaspora.

African American Name-giving

It has been estimated that approximately 100,000 Africans were enslaved and taken directly to South Carolina and Georgia from the Western coast of Africa in the period of one hundred years before the abolition of slave trade in 1800. Even after the slave trade was declared illegal, many Americans effectively continued the stealing of Africans and took them to South Carolina.[22]

Most of these Africans who were forced to leave their homes for South Carolina retained their African speech habits and name practices.[23] All these exhibited a very strong West African influence. Like that of Africa, the practice of giving day names, in either original form or translation, was maintained among the African-American people.[24] However, most Africans who were brought over were unable to keep their original African names when they arrived in America. One of the major reasons is that these names were completely controlled by the slavemasters who did not care to know what their original African names were. To the slave master, slaves were a kind of merchandise and could be given any kind of name that suited their masters. Thus, whoever bought the merchandise gave whatever name he wanted. If one slave was sold five times, he or she might receive five different names. Some of the most common names given to the slaves in those days were "John, Henry, George, Sam, Jack, Tom, Peter, Joe, Mary, Marcia," and others.[25] Those slaves who refused these names publicly were severly punished. Others refused those names in secret. They called themselves by their original African names when they were on the plantations, but not when their masters were there. The names were forced on them not only to be able to call them easily, or to have easier bookkeeping records of the slaves, but mainly to make them forget their African cultural heritage. -They were told they had no history, no culture, no religion, and, that they were sub-human. They were neither allowed to learn to read nor to be converted to the religion of their masters. All of these mentioned above were for the purpose of erasing any memory or tie to their African background and heritage.

After the Emancipation and the American Civil War, African Americans began to reason that since their status had changed, there was a need to change their names, too. They

Cultural Heritage

thought that they were not completely free until they had also changed their names. They adopted general American names, mostly imported from Europe. While many adopted the names of their masters, others just picked up names of people and things in their surroundings. This step was no doubt a strong attempt to forget all memories of the unpleasant past. In these cases, the goal of the masters was achieved. African American naming systems, brought from Africa, began to decline until they almost vanished completely in America. The African American people began to think that they had nothing to do with their fellow brothers and sisters in Africa, because they had been brainwashed that their African brothers hated them and sold them to slavery. It is gratifying that many African-American people have seen the fallacy and the diabolical plan of the slave masters, who were determined to make the slaves forget their cultural heritage from Africa by forcing them to change their original names.

The early missionaries also tried this trick when they arrived in Africa. The innocent Africans were required to change their original African names to biblical or western names whenever they were converted; thus, the missionaries tried to westernize Africans in the name of Christianity. Thank God that Africans have begun to see this and are refusing to change their African names to the western or biblical names.

Many African American people have begun to react to such evil acts by changing to their original African names. Although this is a noble thing to do, yet the African-Americans still have a long way to go in this area of giving African names to their children as a means of perpetuating, or telling the public that they have a cultural heritage. This is indeed very valuable because names are important in Africa as a means of maintaining culture. One is able to tell by African names where a person comes from in Africa. Perhaps if the African American people had kept their original African names from one generation to another, they would have been able to trace the exact place from where their ancestors have come. The slavemasters probably knew this, and therefore forced them to change their names. I think it is now time that African

Cultural Heritage

Americans begin to let the world know that they have a heritage. Such heritage can be expressed in the names they bear and in other walks of life.

The appeal to the African-Americans to claim their cultural heritage through naming their children with African names may seem absurd to many of my readers. However, when one reexamines the importance of name-giving as a vehicle for perpetuating African cultural heritage, such appeal should be understood. Moreover, it appears very reasonable, if we see that other ethnic groups in America, either for one reason or another, continue the naming of their children after their ethnic origin and in their languages. The Italian-Americans are not ashamed to give real Italian names to their children; the German-Americans give actual German names to their children; the Indian-Americans and the Russian-Americans and other ethnic groups do the same thing. Even though the African Americans have been told that they have no historical or cultural heritage, it is now time we dismantle that myth.

African-Americans, therefore, owe it to their children of future generations to pass this cultural, historical and religious heritage on. If they don't, the future generations of the African-American will continue to experience the inferiority complex plaguing African-Americans because of the fact that they were made to believe that they have no culture of any kind.

Any African Americans interested in knowing African names with which to name their children can get them in some of the books sold in Black Bookstores all over the United States. These names can also be learned from many African students and workers, who are all over the United States. The following books discuss African names, their origin, and meaning:

Ogonna Chuks-Odi, *Names from Africa, Their Origin, Meaning and Pronunciation*, edited by Keith E. Baird, Johnson Publishing Company, Inc., Chicago, *1972;*

Handbook of African Names, by Ihe chukwu Madubaike, Three Continents, Washington;

"Names of American Negro Slaves," *American Anthropologist 50*

Cultural Heritage

1948);
Know and Claim Your African Name, by Bektemba Banyika, Dayton, Ohio, Rucker, *1975;*

"Some African Names for Your Baby," *African Progress 1* (June *1971), pp. 36-37;*
African Names from the Ancient Yoruba Kingdom of Nigeria, by Adefunmi, Baba,- Oseijeman, New York, The Yoruba Academy.

---

[1] Ahenafi Kebede, *Roots of Black Music* (Englewood Cliffs: NJ: rentice-Hall, Inc., 1982) 4-5.
[2] Ibid., 5.
[3] Portia K. Maultsby, "Africanism in African-American Music," *Africanism in American Culture*, Joseph E. Holloway (ed. (Bloomington and Indianapolis: Indiana University Press, 1990), 185.
[4] Ibid.
[5] Ibid.
[6] Dena Epstein, *Sinful Tunes and Spirituals* (Chicago: University of Chicago Press, 1977),
[7] Harold Courlander, *Negro Folk Music* (New York: Columbia University Press, 1963), 90.
[8] Kebede, *Roots of Black Music*, 131.
[9] Ibid., 136-137.
[10] Ibid., 138
[11] A.B Pasteur and I.L Toldson, *Root of Souls* (Garden City: NY: Anchor Press, 1982),108.
[12] Ibid. 215.
[13] Mary L. Reilly., ed., *Coast to Coast*, vol. 2, no 3, Spring 1983.
[14] Pasteur and Toldson, *Root of Souls*, 103
[15] Ibid., 239.
[16] Ibid.
[17] John Mbiti, *African Religion and Philosophy* (New York: Praeger Publishers, 1970), 19.
[18] Ibid.,73
[19] Ayoade, "Time in Yoruba Thought," in *African Philosophy*, 77-85.
[20] Mbiti, *African Traditional Religion and Philosophy*, 19
[21] Ibid.
[22] P. Ribert Paustian, "The Evolution of Personal Naming Practices Among American Blacks," *Names*, vol 26, no. 2, June 1978, 180.
[23] Ibid.
[24] Ibid.
[25] Ibid.

Conclusion

It is my hope that my readers have received the message I am trying to pass on. The basic facts are that Africans and African Americans have not always been slaves; that we are the origin of civilization, and that we once ruled the entire world. I have emphasized the fact that survival of Africanism is present in everyday life of the African-American people, even though it is not always recognized. Such African heritage is present in the African-American religious, social attitudes, mannerisms, language, and music. Such heritage can also be seen in the agile and impressive movement of the African-Americans in athletics, ballets, dance, and in their outstanding sense of rhythm.

These are the facts that I think must be known to both young and old. African-American people must seek to know and must know these facts, which tell *what* they were and *who* they are, in order to become whom they want to become.

Just knowing these facts is not enough. African Americans must also be challenged by these facts. Having known that their ancestors were once powerful, they can also be successful now and in the future. African-Americans must teach their children this heritage. They must be told they are the hope for tomorrow. They must encourage their children to attend College. They must not give up when their children refuse to attend College. They must use every means possible to make them go to College, so that Africans and African Americans may be delivered from the present academic monopoly. Africans and African Americans cannot afford to wait for those who do not understand and do not want to understand us, to tell us what we were, what we are, and what we shall be.

African American people must be given great credit for maintaining their African heritage, despite such untold hardship, degradation, brainwashing and dehumanization. It is my hope that this book has enlightened my readers to realize that we have been somebody; we are somebody; and we shall be somebody, because God is with us. African-Americans must therefore be proud of their heritage, keep it, and perpetuate it, for it is a natural gift from God.

SELECTED BIBLIOGRAPHY

Adamo, David T.. *Africa and the Africans in the Old Testament.* San Francisco: Christian Universities Press, 1998, Reprinted by WIPF and Stocks Publisher, Eugene, Oregon.

Awolalu, J. Omosade. *Yoruba Beliefs and Sacrificial Rites.* London: Longman Group Limited, 1979.

Chucks-Orji, Ogonna. *Names from Africa.* Chicago: Johnson Chicago: Johnson Publishing Company, Inc., 1972.

Daramola, Olu and Jeje A. *Asa ati Orisa Ile Yoruba.* Ibadan: Onibon-Oje Press and Book Industries (Nig) LTD., 1975.

Duston, A. G. Jr. *The Black Man in the Old Testament and Its World.* Philadelphia: Dorrance & Company, 1974.

Fauset, A. H. *Black Gods of the Metropolis.* New York: Octagon Books, 1970.

Frazier, F. E. And Lincoln, E. C. *The Negro Church in America.* New York: Shocken Books, 1963.

Herskovits, M. J. *The Myths of the Negro Past.* Boston: Beacon Press, 1958.

Jackson, J. G. *Introduction to African Civilizations,* Secaucus, N.J.: The Citadel Press, 1974.

___. *Man, God and Civilization.* Secaucus, N.J.: Citadel Press, 1972.

Johnstone, R. L. *Religion and Society in Interaction.* Englewood Cliffs: Prentice-Hall, Inc., 1975.

Karenga, Maulana. *Introduction to Black Studies.* Los Angeles: Kawaida Publication, 1985.

Mbiti, J. S. *Introduction to African Religion.* New York: Praeger Publishers, 1975.
_____ *African Religion and Philosophy.* New York: Praeger Publishers, 1970.

McCafi, E. L. *The Black Christian Experience.* Nashville: Broadrnan Press, 1972.

Nketia, Kwabena J. H. *The Music of Africa.* New York: W. W. Norton & Company, Inc., 1974.

Pasteur, A, B. and Toldson, 1. L. *Roots of Souls.* Carden City, N.Y.: Anchor Press, 1982.

Rabotaeu, A. J. *Slave Religion.* New York: Oxford University Press, 1978.

Sertima, Ivan Van. *They Came Before Columbus.* New York: Ran~ dom House, 1976.

Williams, Chancellor. *The Destruction of Black Civilizations.* Chicago: Third World Press, 1976.

Wilmore, Gayraud S. *Black Religion and Black Radicalism.* New York. Orbis Books, Second Edition, 1983.

Wimberly, E. P. *Pastoral Care in the Black Church.* Nashville: Abingdon Press, 1979.

Wright, R. A. Editor. African Philosophy: An Introduction. Washington: University Press of America, 1979.

www.ingramcontent.com/pod-product-compliance
Lightning Source LLC
Chambersburg PA
CBHW070632220426
R18178600001B/R181786PG43193CBX00013B/15